how2become

HOW TO
JOIN THE BRITISH
TRANSPORT POLICE

www.How2Become.com

D1426008

Orders: Please contact How2become Ltd, Suite 2, 50 Churchill Square Business Centre, Kings Hill, Kent ME19 4YU.

You can order through Amazon.co.uk under ISBN 978-1-910602-50-8, via the website www.How2Become.com or through Gardners.com.

ISBN: 978-1-910602-50-8

First published in 2015 by How2become Ltd.

Typeset for How2become Ltd by Anton Pshinka.

Printed in Great Britain for How2become Ltd by:
CMP (uk) Limited, Poole, Dorset.

Disclaimer

Every effort has been made to ensure that the information contained within this guide is accurate at the time of publication. How-2become Ltd are not responsible for anyone failing any part of any selection process as a result of the information contained within this guide. How2become Ltd and their authors cannot accept any responsibility for any errors or omissions within this guide, however caused. No responsibility for loss or damage occasioned by any person acting, or refraining from action, as a result of the material in this publication can be accepted by How2become Ltd.

The information within this guide does not represent the views of any third party service or organisation.

CONTENTS

INTRODUCTION

Hello, and thank you for purchasing *How to Join the British Transport Police.* This guide has been designed to help you prepare for, and pass, the British Transport Police (BTP) selection process.

The selection process to join the police is highly competitive. Approximately 65,000 people apply to join the police every year. But what is even more staggering is that, this year on average, only 550 of these applicants will go on to successfully join the British Transport Police. You could view this as a worrying statistic, or alternatively you could make it your mission to be one of the successful candidates. Armed with our insider's guide, you have already taken the first step to passing the British Transport Police selection process.

The guide itself has been split up into useful sections, to make it easier for you to prepare for each stage of the selection process. As you work your way through this guide, we recommend that you read each section carefully, and take notes as you progress. The best way to approach the selection process is to embark on a programme of 'in-depth' preparation. This guide will show you exactly how to do that!

If you do not spend a decent amount of time preparing, the selection process will not be easy to pass. Furthermore, your preparation must be focused in the right areas. The more comprehensive your preparation, the better your chances of passing will be. The best way to pass the selection process is to develop your own skills and experiences around the core competencies that are required to become a member of the British Transport Police. Many candidates who apply to join the BTP will be unaware that these core competencies even exist.

As you progress through this guide, you will find that the core competencies form the foundations of your preparation. With that being said, the first step is to get hold of a copy of the BTP core competencies. These will usually form part of your application pack, but if they don't, you can obtain a copy of them by visiting the website of the constabulary that you are applying to.

If you need any further help with any elements of the selection process, including the role play activities, written tests or interviews, then we offer a wide range of products to assist you. These are all available at www.how2become.com. We also run a 1-day intensive Police Officer Course. Details of this are available at the website www.PoliceCourse.co.uk.

We wish you every success in your pursuit of joining the British Transport Police.

Best wishes,

The how2become team

The How2become

Attend a 1-day Police Officer course run by former Police Officers at:
www.PoliceCourse. co.uk

CHAPTER 1

How to Pass the
British Transport Police
Selection Process

The role of a British Transport Police Officer

Before you start the application process, it is essential that you learn everything you possibly can about the role of a British Transport Police Officer. There are two reasons for this. Firstly, you need to be 100% certain that this is the right job for you. The Transport Police do not want candidates who will leave only a few months into the job, because *'it wasn't what they expected'*. The second reason is that any prior knowledge you can demonstrate will massively aid you during the selection process. This will be particularly relevant during the interview and assessment centre activities.

What does a Transport Officer do?

In short, the British Transport Police are responsible for policing the railways of the United Kingdom. They ensure that the passengers of trains and customers of railway stations are kept safe at all times. Transport Police are also responsible for policing major events, such as football matches, rugby or public demonstrations. This is particularly important when events such as the Olympic Games are held, where there are large amounts of new or foreign passengers aboard British transport. Transport Police Officers work tirelessly to ensure that all rail passengers are receiving good value for their money, and to help anyone in need of assistance.

If you are an external candidate, then you will generally be applying to the BTP as a Police Community Support Officer (PCSO). As you progress in the career, and pass your probationary period, you will move up the ranks and become a fully recognised British Transport Police Officer.

Let's take a look at the eligibility criteria for joining the British Transport Police.

Eligibility

Before you do decide to apply to the British Transport Police, you will need to make sure that you meet the eligibility criteria. These are as follows:

- **Nationality.** In order to work for the BTP, you must have the right to work and live in the UK without restriction, on a permanent basis.

- **Residency.** Every person who applies to the BTP must have been a resident of the UK for the last 3 years prior to their application date.

- **Age.** You must be at least 18 years old minimum to apply, and 57 years old maximum.

- **Criminal convictions.** You will not be eligible for the BTP if you have any previous convictions, cautions, reprimands or penalty fares (excluding driving penalties). Furthermore, security checks will be conducted on your family, to ensure that they are not involved in any criminal activity. While a family member's criminal background does not mean that you are ineligible to apply, the seriousness of their offence and whether it will bring discredit to the service will be taken into consideration, and could damage your application.

- **Tattoos.** The BTP's attitude towards tattoos depends very much on the nature and location of the tattoo itself. Tattoos on the face, neck and hands are considered unacceptable. Other unacceptable criteria includes:

- *If the tattoo is deemed to undermine the dignity of the applicant.*

- *If the tattoo risks causing offence to the public or other officers.*

- *If the tattoo is too garish, or considered intimidating.*

- **Political.** Applicants who are members of the BNP or other similar parties will be rejected.

- **Financial.** All applicants to the BTP will need to be free from undischarged or unmanageable debt, and must be able to provide a safe and reliable financial history. If you have been registered as bankrupt in the past, then you will only be considered if you are applying 3 years minimum after the discharge of debt.

- **Business.** The BTP are fairly strict on employee business ethics. There are a number of stipulations you will need to abide by, including:

- *You must not hold offices or employment in any other role.*

- *No members of your family or partner can own a shop or anything similar in the area that you would be working in as an officer.*

- *Neither you, your partner or any relative can own an establishment/license which authorises the sale of liquor or betting.*

- **Education.** While there are no specific educational requirements for working with the BTP, this very much depends on the service to which you are applying. Some areas may require you to hold as much as a degree to even have your application considered, while others will require considerably less. You should check with your local service before applying, to ensure you have the qualifications that they are looking for.

Benefits of Working for the BTP

Along with the fact that you'll be working for an organisation that is held in high regard, there are a number of other benefits to working for the British Transport Police. These include:

- A great pension;

- 28 days annual leave;

- An interest free, season ticket loan;

- Opportunity to take part in the 'Cycle to Work' Scheme;

- Child care vouchers and various other financial service benefits.

Core Competencies

The Transport Police core competencies are the basic skills that a candidate must be able to master if he or she is to be capable of successfully performing the role. Throughout this guide I will make continued reference to these competencies. I cannot emphasise how important they are. During the selection process you will be assessed against these core competencies at every stage; therefore it is essential that you are able to learn, understand and demonstrate them to a high standard.

It is important that you obtain a copy of the core competencies prior to completing the application form. You will be tested on these during your application form, the assessment centre and the final interview.

The core competencies for a Transport Police Officer are as follows:

Public Service

This competency requires a candidate to demonstrate a genuine belief in good public service, focusing on what matters to the public and serving the best interests of the community. This is especially important for Transport Police. Passengers have paid to use the rail service, and therefore expect to receive value for their money. As a member of the BTP, you are an essential cog in making sure this happens.

Good public service means being on high alert for when your assistance is required, being polite at all times and being prepared to take action to safeguard rail passengers. You will need to understand the expectations and needs of people from different backgrounds, and must have a firm grasp on the best way to deliver good service to the public. This can often involve working in partnership with other agencies, such as Transport for London.

Adaptability

This competency requires a candidate to demonstrate an openness and positivity towards change, and to be able to adapt rapidly to different ways of working.

You will need a flexible and open approach towards alternative methods of solving problems, and will be required to show an innovative and creative attitude towards new solutions.

Service Delivery

This competency requires a candidate to show that they understand the objectives and priorities of the British Transport Police, and that they can identify how their own work fits into these. You must be able to plan and organise tasks, and take a structured approach to solving problems.

Furthermore, you'll be expected to manage multiple tasks, and show an advanced thought process when prioritising and managing these activities. Your focus should be on the end result of the task, with the aim of working efficiently and accurately to achieve the best possible service.

Professionalism

As a Transport Police Officer, it is extremely important that you are professional and act with integrity at all times. You must take ownership for resolving problems, display courage and resilience when faced with challenging situations, and act on your own initiative to address potential issues. You'll need to act honestly and ethically, and challenge any conduct or behaviour that you identify as being out of line with the ethical values of the British Transport Police.

Finally, you'll need to display a calm and professional attitude when you are under pressure, and must be prepared to step forward and defuse conflict in difficult situations.

Decision Making

Decision making is extremely important for Transport Police Officers. It is vital that you are able to make appropriate and unbiased judgements, to gain an accurate understanding of situations.

You'll need to weigh up a range of possible options, before making clear and justifiable decisions. You'll also be required to review your original decisions, in the light of new information and changing circumstances. All of your decisions and actions should be made with the best interests of the public in mind.

Working with Others

As a Transport Police Officer, it's really important that you have the ability to work co-operatively with others. You'll need to be approachable, positive, a great listener and a great communicator.

You should demonstrate that you are someone who can persuade people, keep them informed and display a compassionate and empathetic attitude to their situation. You will need to treat all people with respect, fairness and dignity, regardless of their background or individual circumstances.

As you can see, the first step on the road to passing the Transport Police selection process is to learn as much as possible about the job role. The great thing about life in the BTP is that you really have the ability to make a difference. Every day, millions of people travel via British trains. Whether they are travelling to and from work, or travelling for leisure purposes, it is your job to make sure that they have a safe and comfortable journey. On cold and dark mornings, this can make all the difference. You will be challenged daily, but your training will provide you with the tools and skills to overcome these difficulties.

Working for the BTP provides you with the opportunity to perform a wide range of roles, and to take personal responsibility for helping others. Dignity and respect are key elements of a Police Officer's working life. There is no greater feeling than bringing a feeling of security to paying customers. Unfortunately, there will often be circumstances where you have to deal with or discipline difficult individuals, who are not operating within the confines of the law. As a Transport Police Officer, you can ensure that justice is delivered by carrying out your job competently, following the correct policies and procedures and filing accurate and concise paperwork.

It is important to remember that, at times, this job can be mentally taxing. You need to ensure that you are prepared for this side of the role. For example, as a member of the BTP you may be required to police or seal off stations in the event of *'one unders'* – where people have perished on the tracks. You may also have to deal with and confiscate drugs, and will also need to handle people who have not paid for their train fare. In order to carry out this part of the role, you will need great courage and sensitivity, and you'll be assessed against this during the selection process. There will also be times when you need to work on the administrative side of the role, and may be required to spend time giving evidence in court.

Finally, you should also be prepared for physical conditions, such as spending long hours on train platforms in extremely cold conditions. Your fitness levels must be good enough to withstand the demands of the job. One of the most common reasons that candidates are rejected from the BTP is due to their lack of physical fitness. Whilst the physical tests are not particularly difficult, you must prepare well in advance for them.

CHAPTER 2

Insider Tips and Advice

The following tips have been carefully put together to increase your chances of success during the Transport Police selection process. Therefore, it is important that you follow them carefully. Whilst some of them will appear obvious, they are still hugely important:

Be Prepared

Regardless of the career for which you are applying, it is vitally important that you prepare yourself fully for every stage of the process. Make sure that you read every single bit of information that you have been given, at least twice, and fully understand what it is that you will be required to do to pass. Go out of your way to prepare.

For example, get a friend or relative to act out a role-play scenario to see how you deal with it. When completing the application form, make sure that you allocate plenty of time to do it neatly, concisely and correctly. Don't leave it until the night before to fill out the form.

In addition to your preparation, it is also very important to believe in your own abilities and take advantage of your potential. For example, if you have applied to the BTP previously and failed, what have you done to improve your chances of success the second time around? Did you work out what areas you failed in, and have you done anything to improve them?

Demonstrate your Values

One of the key aspects of working for the BTP, is behaving with dignity and respect. If you do not believe in equality, fairness and dignity, then you are applying for the wrong job. You'll be expected to demonstrate all of these during the selection process.

The Transport Police are role models within society and people will look to you to set an example. You wouldn't expect to see a police officer bullying or shouting at a member of the public, would you? You will have to use your interpersonal skills to diffuse difficult situations, and you will need to treat people fairly and equally at all times.

During the selection process, your understanding and knowledge of equality and fairness will be tested via the application form, the written tests and during the interview questions. You'll be required to demonstrate that you have a good respect for race and diversity, and that you believe in equal opportunities for everyone.

Physical and Mental Fitness

If you are to be successful in your application as a Transport Police Officer, it is important that you are both physically and mentally fit. In addition to benefitting your health, being physically fit will also improve your self-esteem and confidence. Equally as important are the benefits of having 'a healthy mind', which will help you to learn new skills and develop old ones. The fitter your mind, the easier this will be.

Furthermore, if you are both physically and mentally fit, then you will be able to prepare for longer. You will find that your stamina levels increase, and so will your ability to practice. Make sure you get plenty of sleep in the build up to the assessment day, and ensure that you eat a healthy balanced diet. You will find that if you spend just a week or two eating and drinking the right things, then you will begin to look and feel healthier. Avoid junk food, alcohol and cigarettes during your preparation, and your concentration levels will increase greatly.

Learn About the BTP

This is hugely important for a number of reasons. Firstly, on the application form, you might be asked a question that relates to your knowledge of the role and why you want to join the BTP. As you can appreciate, they want to know exactly what it is about them that has made you apply for the job position. In order to provide a good response to this type of question, you will need to carry out some research. One of the best ways to gain this information is to visit the BTP website, and find out ways that they are helping the community.

If you come into the process with a prior knowledge of the service, then you will demonstrate enthusiasm and commitment towards the cause. Telling an interview panel about current crime trends, statistics and local train issues in your area, will highlight the effort that you have put in your preparation. This will go a long way to helping you gain a position in the service. If you were interviewing a candidate for employment, think about what you would expect them to know. Would you expect them to have undertaken a great deal of research beforehand? If they did have large amounts of prior knowledge, how would you judge them against someone who didn't? You should always attempt to learn as much information as possible about the service, and be extremely thorough in your preparation.

Core Competencies

The BTP core competencies identify how you should behave and perform whilst employed within the service. It is **absolutely fundamental** that you have a good knowledge of all of the competencies required before you start the application process. They are crucial to your success.

Throughout the process you should concentrate on demonstrating the core competencies at every single stage; from your initial application form all the way through to the final interview. The most effective way to achieve this is to use keywords and phrases in your responses. Using words that correspond with these competencies will improve your scores and give you a better chance of success. When you are filling in your application form and preparing for the assessment centre, always make sure that you have a copy of the competencies next to you. These competencies cover a wide range of skills; such as customer focus, problem solving and team work. As we have mentioned, you should be able to find these on any employer's website.

Be Patient and Learn from your Mistakes

The Police Service receive thousands of applications each year, and it takes time to process each one. While you are waiting for them to get in touch with you, use your time wisely and concentrate on the next stage of the selection process.

For example, once you have submitted your application form, start immediate work on your preparation for the assessment centre. The overwhelming majority of candidates will not start their preparation until they receive their results, and as a consequence will miss out on an extra few weeks valuable practice time. Use every bit of your spare time to prepare for the next stage.

If you have previously been through the selection process, and failed, then you need to find out *why* you failed. You should always receive a feedback form informing you of which areas you need to improve upon. There is no point going through the selection process again if you are just going to make the same mistakes.

Understand Diversity

It is fundamentally important that the BTP represents the community that it serves. British communities are diversifying at a furious rate, and the best way to deal with this is to have a multi-cultural police service. Ask yourself the question, 'what is diversity?' If you cannot answer then you will need to find out. Both the application form and final interview will test your knowledge of diversity and multi-culturalism.

Remember that as a Transport Police Officer you must uphold the law fairly in order to protect, respect and help everyone who is travelling. You must also meet with current legislative requirements concerning human rights, race, disability and equality employment laws. Learning, understanding and believing in diversity will be vitally important during the selection process, and is even more important in relation to your role as a police officer.

Never Give Up

If you don't succeed at the first attempt, don't give up. As long as you are constantly improving, there is always a chance that you will succeed. The best way to do this is to look at the stages you have failed and work hard at improving your ability. Don't just sit back and wait for the next opportunity, prepare for it straight away and you'll increase your chances for next time.

Too many people give up on their goals far too easily. Learning to find the positive aspects in negative situations is a difficult thing to do, but is a skill that anyone can acquire through practice and determination. If you really want to achieve your goals, then anything is possible.

During your preparation, set yourself small targets every week. For example, your first week may be used to concentrate on learning the core competencies, and the second week could be used to prepare for your written responses on the application form.

Don't underestimate the value of breaks. If you feel tired or de-motivated at any time, walk away and give yourself some time off. You may find that you come back to the task re-energised, more focused and determined to succeed.

Practice a Mock Interview

Mock interviews are a fantastic way to prepare for the final interview. During the build up to previous interviews, I made a habit of writing down predicted interview questions that I had created for my research. I would then ask a friend or relative to ask me these questions under formal interview conditions. I found this to be excellent preparation, and it certainly served me well during all of my career interviews.

I would estimate that I was successful at over 90% of all of the interviews I attended. I put this success purely down to my detailed preparation.

Finally, I'd also recommend sitting down in front of a mirror and responding to the same set of interview questions. Study your interview technique. Do you slouch? Do you fidget, and do you overuse your hands? If you have prepared fully, you will be amazed at how confident you feel during the actual interview.

In the next section, we'll give you a detailed insight into the best way to complete the BTP Application form. We'll show you what questions to expect, how to answer them, and how to ensure that your application form exhibits all of the core competencies that the Police Service are looking for.

CHAPTER 3

*How to Complete
the Application Form*

Completing the Application Form

The application form is the first stage of the selection process for joining the British Transport Police. You can download and fill in application forms via the British Transport Police website.

During this section, I will provide you with a step-by-step approach to completing a successful application. It is important to point out that I have used a number of the more *common* types of application form question within this section, and therefore these are types of questions that are often asked. Please note that although we have provided these sample questions, they can differ from the actual questions in your application.

When completing your application form, I would recommend that you allow at least five evenings to complete the form, breaking it up into manageable sections. Many candidates will try and complete the form in one sitting, and as a result the quality of their submission will suffer.

On the following pages, I have provided you with tips and advice on how to approach a number of different questions. Please remember that these are provided as a guide only, and that you should base your answers around your own experiences in both your work and personal life. Many of the questions will require you to demonstrate that you have the knowledge, skills and experience as outlined by the personal specification of the job that you are applying for. Therefore, your answers should match these qualities as closely as possible.

Studying the Personal Specification

Your first step should be to study the personal specification of the role. As we have mentioned, the role of a Transport Police Officer is essentially made up of a number of core competencies. You'll find these in your application pack, or on the BTP website. Always make sure that you have a copy of these next to you when you are completing the application form, as you will need to demonstrate as many of these core competencies as possible.

To recap, the core competencies of working for the BTP are as follows:

- Public Service;

- Adaptability;

- Service Delivery;

- Professionalism;

- Decision Making;

- Working with Others.

TOP TIPS!

Helpful Tips

- Make sure that you read the whole of the application form at least twice before preparing your responses, including the guidance notes;

- Read and understand the person specification and the core competencies;

- Try to tailor your answers around the 'core competencies' and include any keywords, phrases or examples that you think are relevant;

- Make sure that you base your answers on actual events that you have experienced either in your work life or personal life;

- Make sure that you fill out the form in the correct ink colour. If you fail to follow this simple instruction, then your form may end up in the bin;

TOP TIPS!

- If there is a specific word count for each question, make sure that you stick to it;

- Make sure that you keep a photocopy of your completed application form before sending it off, as you could be asked questions relating to it during the interview stage;

- Get someone to read over your completed application form to check for any spelling or grammar mistakes;

- Answer all of the questions to the best of your ability. If you leave a question blank, it is highly unlikely that you will move on to the next stage;

- Use examples from your work, social, domestic or educational life to answer the questions. In these examples, they are looking for evidence of specific behaviours which are essential for the job role;

- Be specific: they want to know what YOU said or did to deal with a particular situation. It's important that the examples you provide are from personal experience;

- Write clearly and concisely. They expect your answers to be focused, succinct and fluently written, just like any police report or statement would need to be. This means writing in complete sentences rather than notes or bullet points;

- Pay attention to your handwriting, spelling, punctuation and grammar. Remember that this is a formal application so the use of jargon and slang is unacceptable.

Sample Application Form Questions and Responses

The following sample application form questions will provide you with some excellent tips and advice on how to approach the questions. While you may not necessarily encounter the *exact* questions, you are likely to see very *similar* questions, and this will help you to prepare and plan your answers in advance.

Sample Question 1

What knowledge, skills and experiences do you have that will enable you to meet the requirements of a Transport Police Officer?

---

*'In my previous role as a customer service assistant, I was required to work closely with the general public. Often I was required to provide varied solutions to customer's problems or complaints. It was always important for me to listen carefully to what they had to say and respond in a manner that was both respectful and understanding. (**PUBLIC SERVICE CORE COMPETENCY**)*

*On some occasions I would have to communicate with members of the public from a different race or background. I paid particular attention to helping them understand exactly how I was going to resolve their problems. I was always sensitive to the way they might be feeling. Every Monday morning, my team would hold a meeting to discuss the ways in which we could improve our customer service. During these meetings I would always ensure that I contributed and shared any relevant personal experiences from the previous week. Sometimes during the group discussions, I would find that certain members of the group were shy and not very confident at coming forward, so I sensitively tried to involve them wherever possible. (**WORKING WITH OTHERS CORE COMPETENCY**)*

I remember on one occasion I provided a solution to a problem that had been on-going for some time. I had noticed that customers would often call back to see if their complaint had been resolved, which was time-consuming for the company to deal with. I suggested that we should have a system where customers were called back after 48 hours with an update of progress in relation to their complaint. My suggestion was taken forward and is now an integral part of the company's procedures. I found it quite hard at first to persuade my managers to take on my idea, but I was confident that the change would provide a better service to the public and therefore allow the company to grow'.

Things to remember:

When using examples, don't just think about your work experiences, but look at other aspects of your life too. Try to think of any community work that you have been involved in. Have you ever been in a job of a similar position, or do you/have you worked for a charity or neighbourhood watch? If so, you should find it fairly simple to match your experiences with the competencies of a British Transport Police Officer.

I have now provided a number of sample keywords and phrases that are relevant to each core competency. These will help you to understand exactly what I mean when I say 'match' the core competencies in each of your responses.

Public Service

- 'Focused on the customer at all times to ensure that I delivered an excellent service';

- 'I addressed the needs of the person I was dealing with';

- 'I listened to their viewpoint';

- 'By speaking with them, I was able to build their confidence in my abilities';
- 'I took the time to identify the best way to meet their needs';
- 'I worked alongside other people to ensure that the best service was delivered'.

Openness to change

- 'I was positive about making changes';
- 'I took steps to adapt to the new working practices';
- 'I put in extra effort to make the changes work';
- 'I was flexible in my approach to work';
- 'I searched for alternative ways to deal with the situation';
- 'I took an innovative approach to working with the new guidelines and procedures'.

Service delivery

- 'I consider the organisation's main objectives and aims whilst carrying out my work';
- 'I used an action plan to help me achieve the task';
- 'I was organised in my approach to deal with the situation';
- 'I managed a number of different tasks at once and ensured that my time-management was effective';
- 'I focused on the end result';
- 'I asked for clarification whenever I was unsure'.

Decision Making

- 'I gathered all of the information available before making my decision';

- 'I verified that the information was accurate before using it to make a decision';

- 'I considered all possible options first';

- 'I reviewed my decision once the new information had become available';

- 'I considered the wider implications before making my decision';

- 'I remained impartial at all times';

- 'I considered the confidentiality of the information I was receiving'.

Working with others

- 'I worked with the other members of the team to get the task completed';

- 'I considered the other members of the team and offered my support whenever possible';

- 'I took steps to develop a positive working relationship with the other members of the team';

- 'I fully briefed the other members of the team on what we needed to achieve';

- 'I adapted my style of communication to fit the audience';

- 'I listened to other views and took them into consideration';

- 'I took positive steps to persuade the team to follow my course of action';

- 'I kept the others updated of my progress at all times';

- 'I addressed their needs and concerns immediately';

- 'I treated the other members of my team with respect and dignity'.

You will notice that I have used the word 'I' many times during the above sample keywords and phrases. This is **deliberate!** Remember, it is important to explain what **YOU** did during your responses. Now let's move on to some more sample application form questions and responses.

Sample Question 2

How long have you been thinking about becoming a Transport Police Officer and what has attracted you to the role?

'I have been considering a career as a Transport Police Officer ever since I started my current sales manager job approximately 7 years ago. I enjoy working in a customer focused environment and thrive on providing high levels of service to customers. I have always been aware that the role is demanding and highly challenging but the rewards of such a job far outweigh the difficulties. The opportunity to work as part of an efficient team and work towards providing the community with an effective service would be hugely satisfying'.

Things to remember:

- It is not advisable to state that you have only become interested recently. Candidates who have been seriously thinking about the job for a while will potentially score higher marks;

- In your response, try to demonstrate that you have studied the role carefully and that you believe your skills are suited to being a member of the British Transport Police;

- Read the core competencies and the job description carefully before responding to this question;

- Never be critical of a previous employer.

<hr>

Sample Question 3

What have you done to prepare for this application?

<hr>

'I have carried out a great deal of research to ascertain whether I am suitable for the role, and also to find out whether this career would suit my aspirations. I have studied a great deal in regards to the police officer core competencies to ensure that I can meet the expectations of the BTP.

I have also carried out extensive research prior to filling in my application form, instead of just applying and hoping to be successful. I spoke to several current serving officers at my local station, to ask them about the role and how it affects their life. Finally, I have discussed my intentions with my immediate family, to ensure that I have their full support and encouragement'.

Things to remember:

• At the beginning of this guide, I placed great emphasis on how preparation leads to success. If you have carried out in-depth and meaningful preparation, and can demonstrate this via your responses, then you will massively boost your chances of success. This demonstrates to the BTP that you are serious about wanting the job.

Sample Question 4

Why have you applied for this post and what do you have to offer?

The BTP application form will ask you questions based around your reasoning for applying. You need to answer in conjunction with the personal specification and the job description.

'I believe that my personal qualities and attributes would be suited to that of a police officer within the British Transport Police. I would enjoy the challenge of working in a public service environment that requires a high level of personal responsibility, openness to change and an ability to work with others. I have outstanding levels of commitment, motivation and integrity, which I believe would help the Police Service respond to the needs of the community'.

Things to remember:

• The length of the response that you provide should be dictated by the amount of space available to you on the application form or the specified number of maximum words;

• The form itself may provide you with the facility to attach a separate sheet if necessary. If it doesn't, then make sure that you keep to the space provided;

• The best tip that I can give you is to write down your answer as a rough draft, before writing your response on the actual application form. This will allow you to iron out any mistakes.

Sample Question 5

It is essential that Transport Officers are capable of showing respect for other people, regardless of their background. Please describe a situation when you have challenged bullying, discriminatory or insensitive behaviour. You will be assessed on how positively you acted during the situation, and also on how well you understood what had occurred.

PART 1 – What did you say and what did you do?

ANSWER:

'Whilst working as a sales person for my previous employer, I was serving a lady who was from an ethnic background. I was helping her to choose a gift for her son's 7th birthday when a group of four youths entered the shop. They began to make racist jokes and comments to the lady. I was naturally offended by the comments and was concerned for the lady to whom these comments were directed. Any form of bullying and harassment is not welcome, and I was determined to stop it immediately and protect the lady from any more verbal abuse'.

Things to remember:

- Try to focus your answer on the positive action that you took, illustrating that you understood the situation. Don't forget to include keywords and phrases in your response, which are relevant to the competencies being assessed;

- Make sure that you are honest in your responses. The situations that you provide MUST be ones that you have actively taken part in.

PART 2 – What did you say and what did you do?

'The lady was clearly upset by their actions and I too found them both offensive and insensitive. I decided to take immediate action and stood between the lady and the youths, to try to protect her from any more verbal abuse or comments. I told them in a calm manner that their comments were not welcome and would not be tolerated. I then called over my manager for assistance and asked him to call the police before asking the four youths to leave the shop. I wanted to diffuse the situation as soon as possible. I was confident that the shop's CCTV cameras would have picked up the four offending youths and that the police would be able to deal with the situation. After the youths had left the shop, I sat the lady down and made her a cup of tea whilst we waited for the police to arrive. I did everything that I could to support and comfort the lady, and told her that I would be prepared to act as a witness to the bullying and harassment that I had just seen'.

Things to remember:

- Remember to read the core competencies before constructing your response. Think about what the police are looking for in relation to what YOU say to others, and how you dealt with the situation.

PART 3 – What did you say and what did you do?

'I believe that their behaviour was predominantly down to a lack of understanding, education and awareness. Unless people are educated and understand why these comments are not acceptable, then they are not open to change. They behave in this manner because they are unaware of how dangerous their comments and actions are. They believe it is socially acceptable to act this way, when it certainly isn't'.

Things to remember:

• When describing your thoughts or opinions on how others acted in a given situation, keep your personal views separate. Try to provide a response that shows a mature understanding of the situation.

PART 4 – What would the consequences have been if you had not acted as you did?

'Well, to begin with I would have been condoning this type of behaviour and missing an opportunity to let the offenders know that their actions were wrong. I would also have let the lady down, which in turn would have made her feel frightened, hurt and unsupported. We all need to help prevent discriminatory behaviour. Providing we, ourselves, are not in any physical danger, then we should take positive action to stop it'.

Sample Question 6

Transport Officers are required to work in teams and therefore they must be able to work well with others. Please describe a situation when it was necessary to work with other people in order to get something done and achieve a positive result. During this question you will be assessed on how you co-operated with the other members of the team in completing the task in hand.

PART 1 – Tell us what had to be done.

'Whilst driving along the motorway I noticed that an accident had occurred in front of me. Two cars were involved in the accident and some people in the car appeared to be injured. There were a number of people standing around looking at the crash and I was concerned that help had not been called. We needed to work as a team to call the emergency services, and look after the injured people in the cars'.

Things to remember:

- Make sure that you provide a response to the questions that is specific in nature. Do not fall into the trap of telling them what you 'would do' if the situation was to occur. Tell them what you DID do.

PART 2 – How was it that you became involved?

'I'm not the type of person to sit in the background and let others resolve situations. I prefer to help out where I can and I believed that, in this situation, something needed to be done. It was apparent that people were hurt and the emergency services had not

been called. There were plenty of people standing around but they weren't working as a team to help the victims of the crash'.

Things to remember:

* It is better to say that you volunteered to get involved, than to say you were asked. This shows initiative.

PART 3 – What did you do and what did others do?

'I immediately shouted out loud and asked if anybody was a trained first aid person, nurse or doctor. A man came running over and told me that he worked for the British Red Cross and that he had a first aid kit in his car. He told me that he would look after the injured people but that he would need an assistant. I asked a nearby lady to help him.

I then decided that I needed to call the emergency services and went to use my mobile phone. A man pointed out to me that if I used the orange emergency phone it would get through quicker, and the operator would be able to locate exactly where the accident was. I asked him if he would call the emergency services on the orange phone, as he appeared to know exactly what he was doing.

I noticed a lady sat on the embankment next to the hard shoulder crying. She appeared to be a bit shocked. I asked an onlooker if he would mind sitting with her and talking to her until the ambulance got there. I thought it was important that she felt supported and not alone.

Once that was done, the remaining onlookers and I decided to work as a team to remove the debris lying in the road, which would hinder the route for the oncoming emergency service vehicles'.

Things to remember:

• Provide a response that is both concise and flows in a logical sequence.

PART 4 – How was it decided which way things were to be done?

'I decided to take the initiative and get everyone working as a team. I asked the people to let me know what their particular strengths were. One person was first aid trained and so he had the task of attending to the injured. Everyone agreed that we needed to work together as a team in order to achieve the task'.

PART 5 – What did you do to ensure the team were able to get the result they wanted?

'I took control of a deteriorating situation and got everybody involved. I made sure to ask whether anybody was skilled in certain areas such as first aid and then used the people who had experience, such as the man who knew about the orange emergency telephones. I also kept talking to everybody and asking them if they were OK and happy with what they were doing. I tried my best to co-ordinate people with jobs that I felt were a priority'.

Things to remember:

• Try to include details that demonstrate how your actions had a positive impact on the result.

PART 6 – What benefit did your actions have on the situation, and how did the experience benefit you personally?

'The overall benefit was for the injured people, ensuring that they received treatment as soon as possible. However, I did feel a sense of achievement that the team had worked well together even though we had never met each other before. I also learnt a tremendous amount from the experience. At the end we all shook hands and talked briefly and there was a common sense of achievement amongst everybody that we had done something positive. Without each other we wouldn't have been able to get the job done'.

Sample Question 7

During very difficult circumstances, Transport Officers must be able to remain calm and act logically and decisively. Please describe a situation when you have been in a challenging or difficult situation and had to make a decision where other people disagreed with you. You will be assessed on how positively you reacted in the face of adversity.

PART 1 – Tell us about the situation and why you felt it was difficult.

'Whilst working in my current position as a sales person, I was the duty manager for the day as my manager had gone home sick. It was the week before Christmas and the shop was very busy. During the day the fire alarm went off and I asked everybody to evacuate the shop, which is our company policy. The alarm has gone off in the past, but the normal manager usually lets people stay in the shop whilst he finds out if it's a false alarm. This was a difficult situation because the shop was very busy, nobody wanted to leave and my shop assistants were disagreeing with my decision to evacuate the shop. Some of the customers were irate, as they were in the changing rooms at the time'.

Things to remember:

- For questions of this nature you will need to focus on the core competency that relates to professionalism. Remember to use keywords and phrases in your responses that match the core competencies being assessed.

PART 2 – Who disagreed with you and what did they say or do?

'Both the customers and my shop assistants were disagreeing with me. The customers were saying that it was appalling that they had to evacuate the shop and that they would complain to the head office about it. The sales staff were trying to persuade me to keep everybody inside the shop and saying that it was most likely a false alarm. I was determined to evacuate everybody from the shop for safety reasons, and would not allow anybody to deter me from my aim. The safety of my staff and customers was at the forefront of my mind'.

Things to remember:

- Do not become aggressive or confrontational when dealing with people who disagree with you. Remain calm at all times but be resilient in your actions if it is right to do so.

PART 3 – What did you say or do?

'Whilst remaining calm and in control, I shouted at the top of my voice that everybody needed to leave, despite the sound of the alarm reducing the impact of my voice. I then had to instruct my staff to walk around the shop and tell everybody to leave whilst we investigated the problem. I had to inform one member of staff that disciplinary action would be taken against him if he did not co-operate. Eventually, everybody began to leave the shop. I then went outside with my members of staff, took a roll call and waited for the Fire Brigade to arrive'.

Things to remember:

- Remember to be in control at all times, and remain calm. These are qualities that successful candidates will need to possess.

PART 4 – Tell us how this situation made you feel.

'At first I felt a little apprehensive and under pressure, but I was determined not to move from my position. I was disappointed that my staff did not initially help me but the more I persisted, the more confident I became. This was the first time I had been the manager of the shop so I felt that this situation tested my courage and determination. By remaining calm I was able to deal with the situation far more effectively'.

Things to remember:

- Do not say that you felt angry, and avoid using words that are confrontational;

- By demonstrating that you stayed calm, reflects on your ability to handle difficult situations in an effective and composed manner.

PART 5 – How did you feel immediately after the incident?

'I felt good because I had achieved my aim and I had stood by my decision. It made me feel confident enough that I could do it again and deal with any difficult situation. I now felt that I had the courage to manage the shop better and had proven to myself that I was capable of dealing with difficult situations. I learned that staying calm under pressure significantly improves your chances of a successful outcome'.

Sample Question 8

Transport Officers must deliver an excellent service to the public. Describe a situation when you have had to deal with someone who was disappointed with the level of service they received. Try to use an occasion where you had contact with that person over a long period of time, or on a number of different occasions in order to rectify the problem.

PART 1 – Describe the situation and why you think the person was not happy.

'Whilst working as a sales person in my current job, I was approached by an unhappy customer. He explained to me, in an angry manner, that he had bought a pair of running trainers for his daughter's birthday the week before. When she unwrapped her present on the morning of her birthday, she noticed that one of the training shoes was a size 6 whilst the other one was a size 7. Understandably he was not happy with the level of service that he had received from our company. The reason for his dissatisfaction was that his daughter had been let down on her birthday and as a consequence, he then had to travel back into town to sort out a problem that should not have occurred in the first place'.

Things to remember:

- In order to respond to this type of question accurately, you will need to study and understand the core competency that relates to public service;

- Make sure you answer the question in two parts. Describe the situation first and then explain why the person was not happy.

PART 2 – Explain what you did in response to his concerns.

'Immediately I tried to diffuse his anger by telling him that I fully understood his situation and that I would feel exactly the same if I was in his position. I promised him that I would resolve the situation and offered him a cup of tea or coffee whilst he waited for me to address the problem. This appeared to calm him down and the tone of his voice became friendlier.

I then spoke to my manager and explained the situation to him. I suggested that maybe it would be a good idea to replace the running shoes with a new pair (both the same size) and also refund the gentleman in full as a gesture to try to make up for our mistake. The manager agreed with my suggestion and so I returned to the gentleman and explained what we proposed to do for him. He was delighted with the offer. We then went over to the checkout to refund his payment and replace the running shoes.

At this point I took down the gentleman's address and telephone number, which is company policy for any goods returned for refund or exchange. The man then left the shop happy with the service he had received. The following day I telephoned the gentleman at home to check that everything was OK with the running shoes and he told me that his daughter was delighted. He also informed me that despite the initial bad experience, he would continue to use our shop in the future'.

Things to remember:

• Remember that public service is an important element of the role of a Transport Police Officer. You must focus on the needs of the person you are dealing with at all times.

> **PART 3** – How did you know that the person was happy with what you did?

'I could detect a change in his behaviour as soon as I explained that I sympathised with his situation. The tone of his voice became less agitated and angry, so I took advantage of this situation and tried even harder to turn his bad experience with us into a positive one. When we offered him the refund along with the replacement of the running shoes he appeared to be extremely satisfied. Finally, when I telephoned him the following day he was so happy that he said he would come back to us again, despite the initial poor level of service'.

Things to remember:

- In your response to this part of the question, try to indicate that you followed up on your actions by contacting the person, to see if they were satisfied with what you did for them.

> **PART 4** – If you hadn't acted in the way that you did, what do you think the outcome would have been?

'To begin with, I believe the situation would have become even more heated and possibly untenable. His anger or dissatisfaction could have escalated if my attempts to diffuse the situation had not taken place. I also believe that we would have lost a customer and therefore lost future profits and custom for the company. There would have been a high possibility that the gentleman would have taken his complaint to our head office, trading standards or to the local newspaper.

Customer service is important and we need to do everything we can (within reason) to make the level of service we provide as high as possible. I also believe that our reputation could have been damaged as that particular gentleman could have told friends or colleagues not to use our shop in the future, whereas now, he is more inclined to promote us in a positive light instead'.

Things to remember:

- Demonstrate that you have a clear understanding of what would have happened if you had not acted as you did;

- Study the core competency that is relevant to public service before answering this question;

- Use keywords and phrases in your response from the core competency that is being assessed.

Sample Question 9

Transport Officers must be organised and manage their time effectively. Please describe a situation when you were under pressure to carry out a number of tasks at the same time. Tell us what you had to do, which things were a priority and why.

'Whilst working for a sales company as a manager, I had 4 important tasks to complete on the last working day of every month. These tasks included stocktaking reports, approving and submitting the sales reps' mileage claims, auditing the previous month's accounts, and planning the strategy for the following month's activity.

My first priority was always to approve and submit the sales reps' mileage claims. If I did not get this right or failed to get them submitted on time, the reps would be out of pocket when they received their payslip. This would negatively impact morale and productivity within the office.

The second task to complete would be stocktaking reports. This was important to complete on time, as if I missed the deadline we would not have sufficient stock for the following month, and therefore there would be nothing to sell. This would result in customers not receiving their goods on time.

The third task would be the strategy for the following month. This was usually a simple task, but still important, as it would set out my plan for the following month's activities.

Finally I would audit the accounts. The reason why I would leave this task until the end is that they did not have to be submitted to Head Office until the 14th day of the month, and therefore I had extra time to complete this task, ensuring that I got it right the first time'.

Things to remember:

- Try to demonstrate that you have excellent organisational skills and that you can cope with the demands and pressures of the job.

Sample Question 10

Transport Officers must be capable of communicating effectively with lots of different people, both verbally and in writing. Please explain a situation when you had to tell an individual or a group of people something that they may have found difficult or distressing. You will be assessed on how well you delivered the message and also on what you took into account when speaking to them.

PART 1 – Who were the people and what did you have to tell them?

'The people involved were my elderly next door neighbours. They had a cat that they had looked after for years and they were very fond of it. I had to inform them that their cat had just been run over by a car in the road'.

PART 2 – Why do you think they may have found the message difficult or distressing?

'I was fully aware of how much they loved their cat and I could understand that the message I was about to tell them would have been deeply distressing. They had cherished the cat for years and to suddenly lose it would have been a great shock to them'.

PART 3 – How did you deliver the message?

'To begin with I knocked at their door and asked if I could come in to speak to them. Before I broke the news to them I made them a cup of tea and sat them down in a quiet room away from any distractions. I then carefully and sensitively told them that their cat

had passed away following an accident in the road. At all times I took into account their feelings and I made sure I delivered the message sensitively and in a caring manner'.

PART 4 – Before you delivered your message, what did you take into account?

'I took into account where and when I was going to deliver the message. It was important to tell them in a quiet room away from any distractions so that they could grieve in peace. I took into account the tone in which I delivered the message and I made sure that I was sensitive to their feelings. I also made sure that I would be available to support them after I had broken the news'.

TOP TIPS!

- Read the application form and the guidance notes at least twice before you complete it.

- If possible, photocopy the application form and complete a draft copy first. This will allow you to make any errors or mistakes without being penalised.

- Obtain a copy of the core competencies and have them at your side when completing the form.

- Take your time when completing the form, and set aside plenty of time for each question. I recommend that you spend five evenings completing the application form, breaking it down into manageable portions. This will allow you to maintain high levels of concentration.

- Complete the form in the correct ink colour. Your form could be thrown out for failing to follow simple instructions.

- Be honest when completing the form. If you are unsure about anything, contact the BTP for confirmation.

- Try not to make any spelling or grammar errors. You WILL lose marks for poor spelling, grammar and punctuation.

- Try to use keywords and phrases in your responses, which are relevant to the core competencies.

- Get someone to check over your form for errors before you submit it. If they can't read your application form, then the assessor probably won't be able to either.

- Take a photocopy of your final completed form before submitting it.

- If your form is unsuccessful, ask for feedback. It is important that you learn from your mistakes.

What Happens Next?

Once you have completed and sent off your application form, there will be a wait period before you find out whether or not you have been successful. If you are successful, you will be invited to attend an assessment centre. This will be at a specified centre, at a particular time and date. In the next chapter, we will provide you with some sample material.

It is a good idea to prepare for the assessment centre even before you receive your application result. By starting your preparation early you will be giving yourself a 2-3 week advantage over the other applicants, as 99% of applicants will wait to receive their result before they start to prepare.

CHAPTER 4

Assessment Centre

If your application form is successful, you will be invited to attend an assessment centre. Before attending the assessment centre, ensure that you know how long it will take you to travel to the centre and be sure you know where the location is. Being late will not do you any favours and subsequently, you may not be able to partake in the day. The assessment centre is designed to establish your suitability for a career in the British Transport Police.

You will be required to bring a number of important documents with you in order to confirm your identification:

- A valid passport;

- A driving license;

- A birth certificate, issued within six weeks of birth;

- A cheque book and bank card with three statements and a proof of signature;

- Proof of residence; e.g. council tax, gas, electricity, water or telephone bill.

Make sure that you read all of the information that is given to you, and take along the relevant documents. If you do not, then you won't be able to take part in the day. Finally, you'll need to prepare 100% beforehand, in order to ensure you are ready for the challenges ahead.

How to Prepare for the Assessment Centre

You will have already learnt a considerable amount of job specific information that is relevant to the role of a Transport Police Officer. Once again, the core competencies will form the basis of your preparation, and you should have a copy of them next to you when preparing for each stage of the assessment centre.

> **There are three stages to the BTP assessment centre. These are:**
>
> - Competency based testing, including verbal reasoning, numerical reasoning and an observational ability test;
>
> - A fitness test;
>
> - A competency based interview.

In relation to the competency tests, only you will know your current skill level, and the amount of time necessary to prepare yourself fully for this area. Within the next two chapters you will receive some invaluable advice relating to every area of the assessment, so make sure that you read it carefully and try out the sample test questions.

The Competency Tests

During the assessment centre, you will be asked to undertake a minimum of 3 tests.

These will comprise of:

- A numerical reasoning test;

- A verbal reasoning test;

- An observational ability test.

In this section, we'll look at each of these assessments and provide you with some practice questions, as well as a mock test.

Numerical Reasoning

A Numerical Reasoning test is designed to assess mathematical knowledge through number-related assessments. These assessments will consist of different difficulty levels, and will all vary depending on who you are sitting the test for. Be sure to find out what type of Numerical Reasoning test you will be sitting, to ensure you make the most of your preparation time.

Numerical Reasoning tests can be used to assess the following:

Basic Mental Arithmetic	Critical Reasoning	Critical Interpretation	General Intelligence
Estimations	Speed and Concentration	Financial Reasoning	Data Analysis

Below we have provided example numerical questions that *could* be assessed in your assessment. Please note we have provided an array of different types of numerical questions in order to improve your numerical ability. The questions in this guide are NOT an exact replica of the testing questions in your actual assessment – they are merely written as a way of improving your basic numerical understanding.

Adding Fractions

$$\frac{5}{7} + \frac{3}{5}$$

$$\frac{5}{7} \times \frac{3}{5} = \frac{25 + 21}{35} = \frac{46}{35} = 1\frac{11}{35}$$

Crossbow Method:

The CROSS looks like a multiplication sign and it tells you which numbers to multiply together.

One arm is saying 'multiply the 5 by the 5', and the other arm is saying 'multiply the 7 by the 3'.

The BOW says 'multiply the 2 numbers I am pointing at'. That is 7 times 5.

The answer is 35 and it goes **underneath** the line in the answer.

Subtracting Fractions

$$\frac{4}{7} - \frac{2}{5}$$

$$\frac{4}{7} \times \frac{2}{5} = \frac{20 - 14}{35} = \frac{6}{35}$$

To subtract fractions, the method is exactly the same. The only difference is, you minus the two numbers forming the top of the fraction, as opposed to adding them.

Multiplying Fractions

$$\frac{2}{3} \times \frac{4}{7}$$

$$\frac{2}{3} \times \frac{4}{7} = \frac{8}{21}$$

Arrow Method:

Multiplying fractions is easy. Draw two arrows through the two top numbers of the fraction, and then draw a line through the two bottom numbers (as shown above) and then multiply – simple!

Sometimes the fraction can be simplified, but in the above example, the answer is already in its simplest form.

Dividing Fractions

$$\frac{3}{7} \div \frac{1}{3}$$

$$\frac{3}{7} \times \frac{3}{1} = \frac{3}{7} \times \frac{3}{1} = \frac{9}{7} = 1\frac{2}{7}$$

Most people think that dividing fractions is difficult. But, it's not! Actually, it's relatively simple if you have mastered multiplying fractions.

Mathematicians realised that if you turned the second fraction upside down (like in the above example), and then change the 'divide' sum to a 'multiply', you will get the correct answer – every time!

Simplifying Fractions

$$\frac{24}{30} = \frac{12}{15} = \frac{4}{5}$$

Simplifying Fractions

There are a few steps to follow in order to correctly simplify fractions.

- Can both numbers be divided by 2? If yes, then how many times does 2 go into each number? Write the new fraction.

- Using the new fraction, do the same thing. Can 2 go into both numbers? If yes, divide both numbers by 2.

- If both numbers cannot be divided by 2, then try the first odd number: 3. Can both numbers be divided by 3? If yes, divide both numbers by 3. Do this again until 3 no longer goes into the number.

- If 3 does not go into the numbers again, it doesn't mean it's finished. Try the next odd number: 5, and so on until the fraction can no longer be simplified.

Fractions and Number

What is $\frac{3}{7}$ of 700?

How to work it out:

- $700 \div 7 \times 3 = 300$

Percentages

What is 45% of 500?

How to work it out

- To work out percentages, divide the whole number by 100 and then multiply the percentage you want to find.

- **For example:**

  o 500 ÷ 100 x 45 = 225

  o So, 225 is 45% of 500.

Fractions / Decimals / Percentages

$$\frac{1}{10} = 0.1 = 10\%$$

How to work out fractions into decimals into percentages:

- 0.1 into a percent, you would move the decimal point two places to the right, so it becomes 10%.

- To convert 1/10 into a decimal, you would divide both numbers. For example, 1 ÷ 10 = 0.1.

- To convert 10% into a decimal, you move the decimal point two places to the left. For example, to convert 10% into a decimal, the decimal point moves two spaces to the left to become 0.1.

Volume

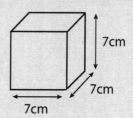

Volume

Length x base x height

- **7 x 7 x 7 = 343**

Areas / Perimeters

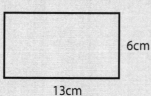

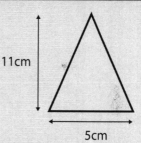

Area of squares/ rectangles

Base x height

- $13 \times 6 = 78$ cm²

Area of triangles

½ base x height

- $11 \times 5 \div 2 = 27.5$

Perimeter

Add all the sizes of each side.

- $6 + 6 + 13 + 13 = 38$

Angles

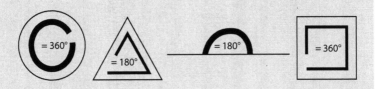

Symmetry

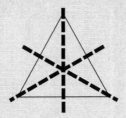

How to work it out:

- To work out how many lines of symmetry a shape has, you need to see where the shape can be folded, in order to create the same reflection.

- Note, an equilateral triangle has 3 lines of symmetry because it can be rotated 3 turns. The triangle would look exactly the same for each rotation.

- **Remember, don't count the same line of symmetry more than once!**

Inputs and Outputs

... —— +12 >—— X 5 >—— 125

How to work it out:

In order to work out the missing number at the start of the sequence, you will need to work backwards.

- When working backwards, you need to do the OPPOSITE.
- For example:
  - $125 \div 5 - 12 = 13$
- You can factor '13' into the equation to make sure you have the correct answer, and the equation works.

Simplifying Equations

Simplify 5w - 6x - 2w - 1x
(5w) (- 6x) (- 2w) (- 1x)
(5w - 2w) = 3w
(-6x - 1x) = -5x
3w - 5x

- The important thing to remember for simplifying equations is to break up the equation (like above).
- The '-' signs and the '+' signs should also be grouped and be on the left side of the number.

Prime Numbers

2	3	5	7	11	13	17	19
23	29	31	37	41	43	47	53
59	61	67	71	73	79	83	89

A prime number is a number that can only be divided by 1 and itself.

- For example, no other numbers apart from 1 and 5 will go into 5.

Factors

Factors are numbers that can be divided into the original number. For example, 6 has the factors of 1 and 6, 2 and 3.

Factors of 12:

Factors are all the numbers that can go into the number.

So, 1 × 12 = 12
2 × 6
3 × 4

So in ascending order, 1, 2, 3, 4, 6 and 12 are all factors of the number 12.

Multiples

- A multiple is a number which is made from multiplying a number in the same pattern.
- For example, the multiples of 2 are: 2, 4, 6, 8, 10, 12, 14 etc.
- Multiples of 15 are: 15, 30, 45, 60, 75 etc.

Speed / Distance / Time

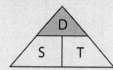 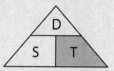 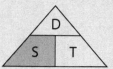

To work out the Distance:

• Distance = Speed x Time

To work out the Time:

• Time = Distance ÷ Speed

To work out the Speed:

• Speed = Distance ÷ Time

Tenths / Hundredths /Thousandths

PLACE VALUE CHART

Millions	Hundred Thousands	Ten Thousands	Thousands	Hundreds	Tens	Ones	Decimal Point	Tenths	Hundredths	Thousandths	Ten-Thousandths	Hundred-Thousandths	Millionths

Stem and Leaf Diagrams

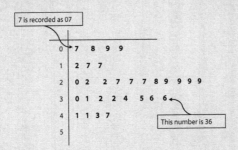

- Stem and leaf diagrams act as a way of handling data.
- These become particularly useful when dealing with large sums of data.
- They are also helpful ways to work out the **mean**, **mode**, **median** and **range**.

Mean / Mode / Median/ Range

Mean

- To work out the mean of a set of data, you add up all the numbers and then divide the total value by the total amount of numbers.

Mode

- The mode is easily remembered by referring to it as the 'most'. What number occurs most throughout the data?

Median

- Once the data is in ascending order, you can then work out what number is the median. In other words, what number is in the middle? If no number is in the middle, use the two numbers that are both in the middle; add them up and divide by 2.

Range

- In ascending order, the range is from the smallest number to the biggest number.

NUMERICAL REASONING TEST

Question 1

A charity arranges a bike race. 120 people take part. 1/3 of the people finish the race in under half an hour. How many people did not finish the race in under half an hour?

Answer

Question 2

What is 3/5 of 700?

Answer

Question 3

There are 4,000 millilitres of water in jugs. If 1 litre is equivalent to 1,000 millilitres, how many litres of water are there?

Answer

Question 4

What is the missing angle?

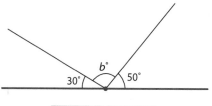

Answer

Question 5

What is 120 multiplied by 13?

Answer

Question 6

Find 60% of £45.

Answer

Question 7

How many lines of symmetry does this shape have?

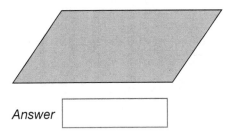

Answer

Question 8

A packet of biscuits weighs 120 g. Find the weight of 9 packets of biscuits.

A	B	C	D
1080 kg	1880 g	1080 g	108 kg

Question 9

A squared field has a perimeter of 72 cm. What is the area of the squared field?

Answer

Question 10

What is 24/48 in its simplest form?

Answer

Study the following chart and answer the four questions that follow.

Bike sales

Country	Jan	Feb	Mar	April	May	June	Total
UK	21	28	15	35	31	20	150
Germany	45	48	52	36	41	40	262
France	32	36	33	28	20	31	180
Brazil	42	41	37	32	35	28	215
Spain	22	26	17	30	24	22	141
Italy	33	35	38	28	29	38	201
Total	195	214	192	189	180	179	1149

Question 11

What percentage of the overall total was sold in April?

A	B	C	D	E
17.8%	17.2%	18.9%	16.4%	21.6%

Question 12

What percentage of the overall total sales were bikes sold to the French importer?

A	B	C	D	E
15.7%	18.2%	18.9%	25.6%	24.5%

Question 13

What is the average number of units per month imported to Brazil over the first 4 months of the year?

A	B	C	D	E
28	24	32	38	40

Question 14

What month saw the biggest increase in total sales from the previous month?

A	B	C	D	E
January	February	March	April	May

Study the following chart and answer the four questions that follow.

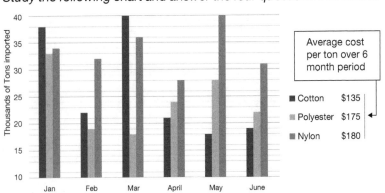

Question 15

What is the mean value for nylon imported over the 6 month period?

A	B	C	D	E
42.5	18.5	33.5	49.5	37.5

Question 16

What is the range for polyester imports across the 6 month period?

A	B	C	D	E
15	21	23	52	51

Question 17

What was the difference in thousands of tons between cotton material and nylon material imports in the first 3 months of the year?

A	B	C	D	E
5	15	24	17	2

Question 18

What was the approximate ratio of polyester and nylon material imports in the first 4 months of the year?

A	B	C	D	E
94:120	94:130	92:110	95:100	94:90

Question 19

The lowest percentage for attendance in Year 7 was 51%. The highest attendance was 100%. The median percent for attendance is 70%. The lower quartile percent was 61% and the upper quartile percent was 90%. Represent this information with a box-and-whisker plot.

Question 20

What is the amount of the lower quartile?

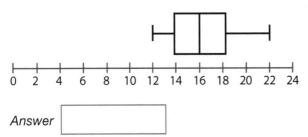

Answer

Question 21

The set of data below shows the results in a year 11 Media mock exam. The marks are out of 100%. The teacher wants to find the mean mark for this test which was given to 68 pupils. Give your answer to 1 decimal place.

Media mock exam (%)	No. of pupils	No. of pupils X media mock exam (%)
10	0	10 x 0 = 0
20	2	20 x 2 = 40
30	3	
40	6	
50	8	
60	11	
70	8	
80	15	
90	12	
100	3	
Totals	68	

The mean mark is:

Question 22

The two way table shown compares pupils' results for GCSE English with GCSE Media grades.

English GCSE Grades	Media GCSE Grades								
	A*	A	B	C	D	E	F	U	Total
A*									
A		2	2	3					7
B		1	3	4				1	9
C			8	10	6	1			25
D				1		2			3
E								1	1
F									
U									
Total		3	13	18	6	3		2	45

The percentage of pupils who received a D grade in Media is approximately what? To the nearest whole number.

Answer [   ]

Question 23

Below is a stem and leaf diagram showing the finishing time, in seconds, of 15 sprinters who took part in a race.

1	8 9
2	0 4 5 6 6 9
3	1 3 5 9
4	0 3 4

What is the median finishing time?

Answer [   ]

Question 24

Using the above stem and leaf diagram, what is the mean finishing time? To one decimal point.

Answer [   ]

Question 25

The head of English created the following table showing the number of pupils in each year group who got a C grade or above in their test.

Year Group	No. of pupils	No. of pupils who achieved a C grade or above in their English test
7	86	56
8	93	48
9	102	72
10	99	52
11	106	85
12	68	56

What is the percentage of pupils in all the year groups combined that got a C grade or above in their test. Give your answer rounded to a whole number.

Answer

Study the following table and answer the following questions.

Company	Company Profit (Annual) (£)	Cost to buy company (£)	Number of employees
A	15,000	18,000	6
B	26,000	24,000	11
C	22,000	20,000	8
D	40,000	40,000	10

Question 26

Using the above table, which company has the lowest annual profit per employee?

A	B	C	D	E
Company A	Company B	Company C	Company D	Company C and D

Question 27

Using the above table, approximately how many more employees would company C have to employ to achieve annual profit of £44,000?

A	B	C	D	E
4	11	8	3	19

Question 28

Using the above table, if company A makes an annual profit of £31,000 the following year, what is the percentage increase? Round it up to 1 decimal place.

A	B	C	D	E
106.7%	94.5%	6.6%	51.6%	103.2%

Question 29

Using the above table, if company D makes an annual profit of £15,000 the following year, what is the percentage decrease?

A	B	C	D	E
105.6%	62.5%	33.5%	101.25%	71%

Study the following line graph and answer the following question.

Number of pupil absences, from five different classes

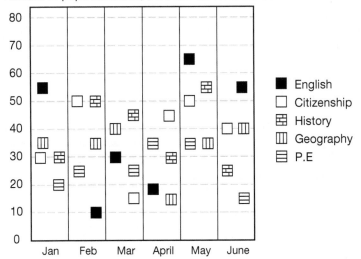

Question 30

What month saw the mode number of pupils to be absent in the one month period, across all five subjects?

A	B	C	D
February	May	June	March

ANSWERS TO NUMERICAL REASONING TEST

Q1. 80

EXPLANATION = 120 (total number of people) ÷ 3 = 40. This is equal to 1/3. Therefore: 40 x 2 = 80.

Q2. 420

EXPLANATION = 700 ÷ 5 x 3 = 420.

Q3. 4

EXPLANATION = there are 1000 millilitres in 1 litre. Therefore, 4000 millilitres is equivalent to 4 litres.

Q4. 100

EXPLANATION = the angle makes a straight line (which in essence, is a half turn of a circle). Therefore the angles would all need to add up to make 180°.   So, 180 – 50 – 30 = 100°.

Q5. 1560

EXPLANATION = 120 x 13 = 1560.

Q6. £27

EXPLANATION = £45 ÷ 100 x 60 = £27.

Q7. 0

EXPLANATION = this shape is a parallelogram, and these shapes do not contain a line of symmetry. No matter where you draw the reflection line, the shape cannot be reflected symmetrically.

Q8. C = 1080 g

EXPLANATION = 120 x 9 = 1080 g. Pay attention to the measurements; the question is in grams (g), so therefore your answer should also be in grams, unless stated otherwise.

Q9. 324 cm²

EXPLANATION = the key thing to remember is that the shape is a square (the sides will be the same length). If the perimeter of the shape is 72 cm, then 72 needs to be divided by 4 (4 sides). So, 72 ÷ 4 = 18. Each length of the side is 18 cm, and to work out the area = 18 x 18 = 324 cm².

Q10. ½

EXPLANATION = 24/48, both numbers can be divided by 24. 24 goes into 24 once, and goes into 48 twice. Therefore it gives the fraction of ½.

Q11. D = 16.4

EXPLANATION = to work out the percentage overall total that was sold in April, divide how many bikes were sold in April (189) by the total (1149) and then multiply it by 100. (189 ÷ 1149 x 100 = 16.4).

Q12. A = 15.7%

EXPLANATION = to work out the overall percentage total that was sold to France, divide how many bikes were sold to France (180) by the total (1149) and then multiply it by 100. (180 ÷ 1149 x 100 = 15.66). Rounded up to 1 decimal place = 15.7.

Q13. D = 38

EXPLANATION = to work out the average number of units per month imported to Brazil over the first 4 months of the year, you add up the first 4 amounts (Jan-April) and then divide it by how many numbers there are (4). So, (42 + 41 + 37 + 32 = 152 ÷ 4 = 38).

Q14. B = February

EXPLANATION = to find out the biggest increase in total sales from the previous month, you should calculate the difference between the totals for each of the month, and then work out which has the biggest increase. Between January and February, there was an increase by 19. None of the other months have a bigger increase, and therefore February is the correct answer.

Q15. C = 33.5

EXPLANATION = nylon material = 34 + 32 + 36 + 28 + 40 + 31 = 201 ÷ 6 = 33.5.

Q16. A = 15

EXPLANATION = to work out the range, find the smallest and highest number of polyester imports (18) and (33). So, 33 – 18 = 15 (thousands).

Q17. E = 2

EXPLANATION = to work out the difference, add up the first 3 months for cotton (38 + 22 + 40 = 100). Add up the first 3 months for nylon (34 + 32 + 36 = 102). So, the difference between cotton and nylon = 102 – 100 = 2 (thousands).

Q18. B = 94:130

EXPLANATION = 94,000:130,000. Divide both numbers by 1000 to give you 94:130.

Q19. Your box and whisper plot diagram should look like this:

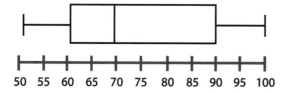

Q20. 14

EXPLANATION = the lower quartile range is the first line that forms the box. So, the correct answer would be 14.

Q21. 67.2%

EXPLANATION = add up the "number of pupils multiplied by media mock exam" and then divide it by the "number of pupils".

Media mock exam (%)	No. of pupils	No. of pupils X media mock exam (%)
10	0	10 x 0 = 0
20	2	20 x 2 = 40
30	3	30 x 3 =90
40	6	40 x 6 = 240
50	8	50 x 8 = 400
60	11	60 x 11 = 660
70	8	70 x 8 = 560
80	15	80 x 15 = 1200
90	12	90 x 12 = 1080
100	3	100 x 3 = 300
Totals		

So, 4570 ÷ 68 = 67.2%.

Q22. 13%

EXPLANATION = number of pupils who received a D grade in Media = 6.

Total number of pupils = 45.

So, 6 ÷ 45 x 100 = 13.333%. To the nearest whole number = 13%.

Q23. 29 seconds

EXPLANATION = 'median' simply means 'middle'. So, what number is in the middle? Using the data in ascending order, you will notice that 29 (seconds) is the median/middle number.

Q24. 30.1 seconds

EXPLANATION = to work out the mean number, add up all the numbers and then divide it by how many numbers there are.

So, 452 ÷ 15 = 30.133. To one decimal point = 30.1.

Q25. 67%

EXPLANATION = add up total number of pupils = 554.

Add up the number of pupils who achieved a C grade or above in English = 369.

To work out the overall percentage = 369 ÷ 554 x 100 = 66.6%.

To the nearest whole number = 67%.

Q26. B = Company B

EXPLANATION = simply divide the annual profit for each company by the number of employees, and see which company has the lowest profits.

Q27. C = 8

EXPLANATION = 44,000 ÷ 2750 = 16. That is 8 more than what they have already.

Q28. A = 106.7%

EXPLANATION = 31,000 – 15,000 = 16,000.

So, 16,000 ÷ 15,000 x 100 = 106.666% = 106.7%

Q29. B = 62.5%

EXPLANATION = 40,000 – 15,000 = 25,000.

So, 25,000 ÷ 40,000 x 100 = 62.5%.

Q30. B = May

EXPLANATION = you need to add up all of the subjects for each month. January = 170, February = 170, March = 155, April = 145, May = 240, June = 175. Therefore the mode (the most) in one given month is in May.

TOP TIPS FOR NUMERICAL REASONING!

Helpful Tips

- Make sure you practice your mathematical skills. You will find the numerical reasoning test difficult if you are not great at maths. Practice your adding, subtracting, multiplying and dividing. Also practice mathematics including fractions, percentages and ratios.

- Try practising numerical test questions in your head, without writing down your workings out. This is very difficult to accomplish, but it is excellent practice for the real test. Also, practice numerical reasoning tests without a calculator, as you do not want to become completely reliant on the use of a calculator.

- If you are permitted to use a calculator, make sure you know how to use one!

- Questions will often require you to identify what mathematical formulae is being used (division, percentage, ratio etc). Before you answer the question, carefully read what the question is asking you! Be sure to understand what you need to work out, before attempting to answer the question.

- Practice is key. The more you practice your mental arithmetic and other mathematical formulae; the easier it becomes. This is why we have provided you with lots of sample questions for you to work through. The more you practice these tests, the more likely you are to feel comfortable and confident with the questions. Remember, practice makes perfect!

- Make sure you pay attention to detail. Recognising units, and measurements and other important mathematical formulas is crucial when it comes to your answer. If a question asks you to write your answer in centimetres, and you write your answer using millimetres, this is a careless mistake that is going to cost you easy marks!

Verbal Reasoning

The second of the competency related assessments will be the Verbal Reasoning test. Verbal Reasoning tests are used to determine a number of different aspects about a candidate.

This includes:

- How well you take in written information;

- Your understanding of grammar, spelling and punctuation;

- Your ability to choose between correct and false information;

- How well you understand the meanings of words;

- Your knowledge of different literary terminology.

ODD ONE OUT

Identify which word is the odd one out.

Question

A – Desk
B – Shelf
C – Cupboard
D – Chair
E – Wood

How to work it out

- The odd one out is 'wood'.
- All of the other words are objects commonly made from wood. So wood is the word linking these words together.

Answer

E – Wood

WORD JUMBLES

*In the sentence, the word outside the brackets will only go with three of the words inside the brackets, in order to make a longer word. Which **ONE** word will it **NOT** go with?*

Question

	A	B	C	D
Un	(adaptable	able	appropriate	afraid)

How to work it out

- Unadaptable
- Unable
- Unafraid
- **Unappropriate** is not a word. The correct term would be 'inappropriate'.

Answer

C – Appropriate

COMPLETE THE SENTENCE

Complete the following sentence by adding in the correct words in the missing spaces.

Question

Which word makes the best sense in the following sentence?

The mechanic worked on the car for 3 hours. At the end of the 3 hours he was _____ .

A	B	C	D
Home	Rich	Exhausted	Thinking

• The only word that makes sense would be 'exhausted'.

Answer

C = Exhausted

WORD FAMILIES

In each question, there are four or five words, your job is to pick out the word that links all the other words together.

EXAMPLE:

A	B	C	D
Trousers	Clothing	Shirt	Skirt

How to work it out:

- You need to work out which word can group all of the other words to form a word family.

For the above example, 'clothing' is the word that links trousers, skirt and shirt, so therefore the correct answer would be B.

Answer

B = clothing

ANTONYMS / SYNONYMS

Work out what word means the opposite or the same as the word stated.

EXAMPLE:

Beautiful

How to work out the antonym:

- Antonym means opposite, so you need to find a word that means the opposite to beautiful. For example, ugly.

How to work out the synonym:

- To work out the synonym for the above example, you need to find a word that means 'the same as'. For example, stunning.

COMPOUND WORDS

In each of the following questions, find the two words, one from each group, that together make a new, real word. The word from the group on the left always comes first.

(man bend sauce)   (tomato pan den)

How to work it out:

- In order to work out these types of question, you need to find a word from the left group to start off the new word.

- Eliminate the answers you know to be incorrect.

- You should realise that 'sauce' and 'pan' can be put together to make the new word 'saucepan'.

Answer

Saucepan

ALPHABET PATTERNS

In each of the following questions, find the letters that best complete the series. The alphabet has been provided to assist you.

A B C D E F G H I J K L M N O P Q R S T U V W X Y Z

PW   [ ]   XO   BK   FG   JC

A – TS
B – ST
C – RS
D – TU

How to work it out:

- Let's take the first letter of each group and work out how it is progressing. Let's start with the third group (XO) because you need to work out a common pattern.

- You should notice that the first letter is moving up the alphabet four places (4 spaces from 'x' = 'b'). Once the pattern reaches the end, it begins back at the start of the alphabet.

- So to work out the first letter of the second group, take the first group and its starting letter 'p', and add four spaces (P + 4 = T).

- Now work out how the second letter is progressing.

- You should notice that the sequence is moving down the alphabet 4 spaces. (O = K = G = C).

- So the second group needs to go down from W, 4 spaces = S.

- So therefore the correct answer is TS.

Answer

A = TS

HIDDEN WORDS

A word is hidden amongst the sentence. It has four letters and is hidden at the end of one word and the beginning of the next word. What is the hidden word?

EXAMPLE:

I need ice cold drinks during the summer time.

How to work it out:

- You need to find the hidden four letter word that is part of the ending of one word, and the beginning of the next.

- For this example, you need to pay attention to 'need' and 'ice'.

'nee**D ICE**'

Answer

Dice

CONNECT THE WORDS

In each question, there are two pairs of words. Only one of the answers will go equally well with both of these pairs.

(Look out for meanings of the words and other possibilities of how another word could be used in that situation).

Question

(fall tumble)   (journey   outing)

A	B	C	D
Travel	Trip	Trap	Drop

- 'Travel' would not be appropriate because it doesn't fit with the first set of words.
- 'Trap' doesn't work because it doesn't fit with the second set of words.
- 'Drop' doesn't work because it doesn't fit with the second set of words.

Answer

B = trip (meaning to fall or stumble) or (taking a trip somewhere).

CORRECT LETTERS

The same letter must be able to fit into both sets of brackets [?] in order to complete the word in front of the bracket, and begin the word after the bracket.

Question

Happ   [?]   ellow
Wh   [?]   awn

A	B	C	D
W	H	Y	N

- The only letter that could fit inside the bracket in order to make 4 words is = Y.
- Happ**y**, **y**ellow, wh**y**, **y**awn

Answer

C = Y

VERBAL REASONING TEST

Question 1

What word pair has the most similar relationship to…

Colour : Spectrum

A	B	C	D
Verse : Rhyme	Waves : Sound	Tone : Scale	Nature: Atmosphere

Question 2

Which **one** word has a meaning that extends to or includes the meaning of all the other words?

A	B	C	D	E
Gymnastics	Swimming	Running	Training	Football

Question 3

A word is hidden amongst the sentence. It has four letters and is hidden in one word and at the beginning of the next word. What is the hidden word?

For the last time, I will not tell you again.

Answer

Question 4

Which word does not have a similar meaning to – imaginary?

A	B	C	D
Mythical	Fictional	Illusive	Fickle

Question 5

In the line below, the word outside of the brackets will only go with three of the words inside the brackets to make longer words. Which ONE word will it NOT go with?

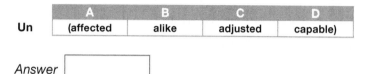

	A	B	C	D
Un	(affected	alike	adjusted	capable)

Answer

Question 6

Which of the following words is the odd one out?

A	B	C
Forever	New	Fresh

Question 7

Which word is the odd one out?

A	B	C	D	E
Ostrich	Parrots	Penguins	Dodo	Owls

Question 8

In the line below, the word outside of the brackets will only go with three of the words inside the brackets to make longer words. Which **one** word will it **not** go with?

	A	B	C	D
Un	(assuming	admired	usual	draught)

Answer

Question 9

Four of the five sentences have the same meaning. Which **one** sentence has a **different** meaning?

A – Mike spent £180 during his shopping trip.

B – During his shopping trip, Mike spent £180.

C – The shopping trip cost Mike £180.

D – Mike made £180 from his shopping trip.

E – A total of £180 was spent on Mike's shopping trip.

Answer [　　　　　　]

Question 10

In the line below, the word outside of the brackets will only go with three of the words inside the brackets to make longer words. Which **one** word will it **not** go with?

	A	B	C	D
An	(tarctic	aerobic	ability	droid)

Answer [　　　　　　]

Question 11

Fill in the missing word so that the sentence reads correctly.

He ____the telephone and then _____ it to his mother.

A	B	C	D
Heard / shouted	Answered / spoke	Picked / threw	Answered / passed

Question 12

Fill in the missing word so that the sentence reads correctly.

_____ *going to be in big trouble when they get home.*

A	B	C	D
Thair	There	Their	They're

Question 13

In the line below, the word outside of the brackets will only go with three of the words inside the brackets to make longer words. Which **one** word will it **not** go with?

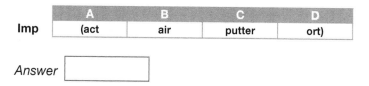

	A	B	C	D
Imp	(act	air	putter	ort)

Answer [   ]

Question 14

Which of the following is the odd one out?

A	B	C	D
Trumpet	Violin	Harp	Guitar

Question 15

The following sentence has one word missing. Which **one** word makes the best sense when placed in the sentence?

A submarine is a vehicle that is _____ of independent operation underwater.

A	B	C	D	E
Evolved	Built	Capable	Designed	Submersible

Question 16

Four of the five sentences have the same meaning. Which **one** sentence has a **different** meaning?

A – It was a little girl who was pushed over by the tall boy.

B – The tall boy pushed over a little girl.

C – The little girl pushed over the boy.

D – The little girl fell over as a result of being pushed by the tall boy.

E – The tall boy got into trouble for pushing over a little girl.

Answer

Question 17

In the line below, the word outside of the brackets will only go with three of the words inside the brackets to make longer words. Which **one** word will it **not** go with?

	A	B	C	D
Im	(age	agine	moral	significant)

Answer

Question 18

The following sentence has one word missing. Which **one** word makes the best sense when placed in the sentence?

The man _____ he wanted to go home.

A	B	C	D	E
Chose	Needed	Decided	Ran	Boasted

Question 19

The following sentence has one word missing. Which **one** word makes the best sense when placed in the sentence?

The weather forecaster informed the public of the _____ rain.

A	B	C	D	E
Likelihood	Chance	Dry	Need	Potential

Question 20

Which of the following words is the odd one out?

A	B	C	D
Circle	Rectangle	Sphere	Triangle

Question 21

Which letter is missing from the following words?

HER (_) RAG and **BLUR (_) ALL**

A	B	C	D
B	S	T	U

Question 22

Which of the following is the odd one out?

A	B	C	D	E
Rose	Lily	Daisy	Petal	Sunflower

Question 23

Which letter is missing from the following words?

FEE (_) *ARE* and *PLEA* (_) *ATE*

A	B	C	D
D	L	S	Y

Question 24

Which of the following is the odd one out?

A	B	C	D
Now	Cow	Low	How

Question 25

In the line below, the word outside of the brackets will only go with three of the words inside the brackets to make longer words. Which ONE word will it NOT go with?

	A	B	C	D
In	(decisive	reference	destructible	convenience)

Answer [   ]

Question 26

Which four letter word can be placed at the **end** of the following words, in order to create four new words?

King   **Parent**   **Adult**   **Liveli**

Answer [   ]

Question 27

Which four letter word can be placed at the **end** of the following words, in order to create four new words?

Accept   Charit   Foresee   Float

Answer

Question 28

If the following words were placed in alphabetical order, which one would be third?

A	B	C	D
Delightful	Delicious	Delayed	Delicate

Answer

Question 29

The following sentence has one word missing. Which **one** word makes the best sense when placed in the sentence?

He needed to be _____ for what he had done.

A – Helped

B – Reprimanded

C – Stopped

D – Maintained

E – Custody

Answer

Question 30

Which of the following words is the odd one out?

A	B	C	D	E
Cup	Fork	Knife	Teaspoon	Spoon

Question 31

Which letter is missing from the following words?

Taugh[?]   [?]hing   tigh[?]   [?]ile

A – T

B – S

C – E

D – N

Answer [   ]

Question 32

Which letter is missing from the following words?

Skate[?]   [?]ace   clove[?]   [?]after

A – E

B – S

C – P

D – R

Answer [   ]

ANSWERS TO VERBAL REASONING TEST

Q1. C = Tone : Scale

EXPLANATION = for this type of question, you need to work out what two words have the most similar meaning to the two words shown. 'Colour' and 'spectrum' both can be related to 'tone' and 'scale'. Colours have different tones and can be defined on a scale i.e. light and dark; just like a spectrum has a scale and tones of colour.

Q2. D = training

EXPLANATION = 'training' is the one word that groups all of the other words together. Gymnastics, swimming, running and football are all types of training exercises for athletic sport.

Q3. Fort

EXPLANATION = '**for t**he'.

Q4. D = fickle

EXPLANATION = fictional, illusive and mythical are all words that relate to 'imaginary'. 'Fickle' does not carry the same connotations as these words and therefore does not have a similar meaning.

Q5. D = capable

EXPLANATION = if you were to put 'un' with the words 'affected', 'alike' and 'adjusted', you would get: unaffected, unalike and un-adjusted. However, if you tried to put 'un' with 'capable', it would not be grammatically correct. Therefore answer D does not go with the word outside the bracket.

Q6. A = forever

EXPLANATION = 'forever' is the odd one out because both 'new' and 'fresh' have a similar meaning.

Q7. D = dodo

EXPLANATION = all of the other words refer to birds that are not extinct.

Q8. D = draught

EXPLANATION = if you were to put 'un' with the words 'assuming', 'admired', and 'usual', you would get: unassuming, unadmired and unusual. However, if you were to put 'un' with 'draught', this would not be grammatically correct.

Q9. D = Mike made £180 from his shopping trip.

EXPLANATION = the other four sentences refer to Mike spending money, therefore answer option D (Mike made £180 from his shopping trip) means something different.

Q10. C = ability

EXPLANATION = if were to put 'an' with 'tarctic', 'aerobic' and 'droid', you would get: 'Antarctic', 'anaerobic' and 'android'. However, if you were to put 'an' with 'ability', this would not be grammatically correct.

Q11. D = answered / passed

EXPLANATION = He **answered** the telephone and then **passed** it to his mother.

Q12. D = they're

EXPLANATION = in order to find the missing word, you need to work out the sentence structure. Is it in past tense, present tense or future tense? The word that is grammatically correct for this sentence is 'they're'. So, the sentence would read 'they're (they are) going to be in big trouble when they get home'.

Q13. C = putter

EXPLANATION = impact, impair, import. Therefore the word that does not fit with (imp) is 'putter'. Impputter is not a word, and therefore does not fit with the word outside the brackets.

Q14. A = trumpet

EXPLANATION = trumpet is the only instrument listed that requires you to play using your mouth. The other instruments require you to play the instrument using your hands.

Q15. C = capable

EXPLANATION = the word that would best fit the sentence is 'capable'. So, the sentence would read 'a submarine is a watercraft capable of independent operation underwater'.

Q16. C = the little girl pushed over the boy.

EXPLANATION = the sentence 'the little girl pushed over the boy' has the opposite meaning to all of the other sentences, therefore this sentence is the odd one out.

Q17. D = significant

EXPLANATION = if you were to put 'im' with 'age', 'agine' and 'moral', you would get: 'image', 'imagine' and 'immoral'. However, if you were to put 'im' with 'significant', this would be grammatically incorrect.

Q18. C = decided

EXPLANATION = the correct word is 'decided'. So, the sentence would read 'the man decided he wanted to go home'.

Q19. E = potential

EXPLANATION = the word that is needed in order to make the sentence grammatically correct is 'potential'. So, the sentence would read 'the weather forecaster informed the public of the potential rain'.

Q20. C = sphere

EXPLANATION = 'sphere' is the odd one out because all of the other words refer to 2D shapes. A sphere is 3-dimensional.

Q21. A = B

EXPLANATION = *herb, brag, blurb* and *ball*.

Q22. D = petal

EXPLANATION = 'petal' is the odd one out because all of the other words refer to 'types' of flowers, whereas a 'petal' is part of a flower

Q23. A = D

EXPLANATION = *feed, dare, plead* and *date*.

Q24. C = low

EXPLANATION = low is the odd one out, because it is pronounced differently from the other three words.

Q25. B = reference

EXPLANATION = if you were to put the word 'in' with the words 'decisive', 'destructible' and 'convenience', you would get: 'indecisive', 'indestructible' and 'inconvenience'. However, if you were to put the word 'in' with the word 'reference', this would be grammatically incorrect.

Q26. Hood

EXPLANATION = king*hood*, parent*hood*, adult*hood* and liveli*hood*.

Q27. Able

EXPLANATION = accept*able*, charit*able*, foresee*able* and float*able*.

Q28. B = delicious

EXPLANATION = in alphabetical order, the words would read as follows: *delayed, delicate, delicious* and *delightful.* So the third word in the sequence would be 'delicious'.

Q29. B = reprimanded

EXPLANATION = the sentence would best read as follows: '*He needed to be* **reprimanded** *for what he had done'.*

Q30. A = cup

EXPLANATION = 'cup' is the odd one out because all of the other words are types of cutlery, whereas a 'cup' is an item of crockery.

Q31. A = T

EXPLANATION = *taught, thing, tight* and *tile.*

Q32. D = R

EXPLANATION = *skater, race, clover* and *rafter.*

TOP TIPS FOR VERBAL REASONING!

Helpful Tips

When taking Verbal Reasoning tests, some people like to work on the questions they find most difficult first. Some people prefer to leave the harder questions to last. Pick a way that you feel comfortable with, and use it throughout your Verbal Reasoning test.

1. Accuracy is key. You need to remain as accurate as possible to ensure successful marks. That's why it is important to fully comprehend the questions and understand what is being asked.

2. Make sure that you take the practice questions under timed conditions. This will help to better your overall performance by allowing you to practice under similar conditions to that of the real test.

3. Make sure you read the question very carefully. Some questions are designed to trick you, so you need to fully understand what the question is asking you to do, before you answer it. We recommend that you read the question at least twice before attempting to answer it.

4. Practice as many different *types* of verbal reasoning questions as you can. Within this guide we have provided you with several different question types, in order to increase your understanding and enhance your performance. Please note, the question types within this guide are not exhaustive, they are merely a way to indicate the most common types of question found in the BTP Verbal Reasoning Test.

5. Practice a variety of difficulty levels. If you are undergoing practice questions and are finding them relatively easy, why not practice more difficult questions? This will allow you to boost your confidence and enhance your skills. If you practice a variety of difficulty levels, you will be ready to tackle any type of Verbal Reasoning question that you encounter in the assessment.

Observational Test

The last of the 3 tests that you'll have to take is an observational test. The observational test will examine your ability to remember key details and information, with a limited timeframe in which to do it.

The format of the observational test is prone to changing, but you are most likely to be shown 1 or 2 short video clips, and will then be asked to answer questions on each one. The questions will test you on how much you remember about what you saw in the video clip, and will ask you things such as, *'what colour was the woman's dress?'* or *'how many cars were there?'*.

As an aspiring Transport Police Officer, you will need to be someone with a keen eye for detail, who can spot potential danger or trouble before it becomes a risk. You'll also be expected to remember details, as this could later prove vital in a court or legal situation.

The key to passing the observational test is to train your memory to remember particular details. Below we've included a number of sample exercises, to give you some idea of how you can do this.

Example 1 Memory Test

Take a look at the grid below. Study the grid for a total of 2 minutes, before covering it up and then writing down as many words as you can remember.

account	noon	section	tube	corner	fruit
bear	folder	pottery	extract	thought	music
dew	office	point	store	wheel	life
brother	paper	rest	syrup	colour	belt
mind	thunder	hole	problem	magic	safe

The more of these questions you practice, the more your memory will improve. This exercise tests almost the exact same skills as the observational test. The difference, of course, is that this exercise is significantly easier. Here you are only trying to remember words, which are laid out in a structured format. The details that you will need to remember from the observational videos are not so obvious.

Now, take a look at another image, and then try to answer the question below. There may be 1 or more answers to the question, so pay close attention.

Example 2 Memory Test

What did you see in the picture?

1. A lorry

2. A train

3. A crane

4. A bridge

5. Two way traffic

Answer: A crane and a bridge.

Hopefully the above exercises should give you some idea of what to expect from the test. As we have mentioned, while the test will most likely be taken in video format, attempting to remember the details of 'busy' images will help you enormously when preparing.

Please note: The questions that we have provided you are not the exact questions that you will encounter in the test. They are simply examples, to give you an idea of what to expect and help you prepare for the skills and attributes you may be assessed on.

OBSERVATIONAL ABILITY TEST

Question 1

Study the picture for 3 seconds, and then cover it up.

What did you see in the picture?

1. A car

2. A bus

3. A pedestrian

4. A cyclist

5. A truck

Answer

Question 2

Study the picture for 3 seconds, and then cover it up.

What did you see in the picture?

1. Four cars

2. A lorry

3. A road sign

4. A road junction

5. A motorcyclist

Answer [   ]

Question 3

Study the picture for 3 seconds, and then cover it up.

How many trains did you see in the picture?

Answer

Question 4

Study the picture for 3 seconds, and then cover it up.

What did you see in the picture?

1. Motorway sign for junction 31

2. Motorway sign for junction 30

3. A caravan being towed

4. A bus

5. A lorry

Answer

Question 5

How many *fire stations* have the area code *(01814)*?

Key

🏥 Hospitals   ✈ Airports   📚 Libraries   🛒 Shops   ⊠ Post offices   🎬 Cinemas

🔥 Fire stations   🍴 Cafes   Ⴢ Bars   🔧 Repair shops   ✂ Tailors

🚚 Shipping companies   🔧 Plumbers

(01982) 867725 ⊠ (01757) 557959 🍴 (01977) 109544 🛒 (01083) 629469 🍴 (01066) 515597 🛒
(01910) 690890 Ⴢ (01757) 868588 🏥 (01066) 097888 🍴 (01910) 290338 📚 (01814) 623704 ✂
(01083) 645620 ✈ (01066) 351315 🍴 (01757) 209321 Ⴢ (01814) 072745 🏥 (01814) 230071 🔧
(01982) 449585 🍴 (01424) 037342 🍴 (01814) 707490 🔥 (01083) 784235 📚 (01860) 376579 Ⴢ
(01424) 480870 🔥 (01499) 483418 🏥 (01910) 739074 🔧 (01977) 993609 🎬 (01499) 021761 🚚
(01860) 638818 📚 (01066) 559078 🚚 (01066) 229519 ⊠ (01757) 642417 🔧 (01910) 338863 🔥
(01757) 042680 ✂ (01066) 507994 🎬 (01757) 939551 ✈ (01860) 640527 🏥 (01860) 174685 ✈
(01982) 601123 ✈ (01814) 004051 🍴 (01977) 726148 🚚 (01066) 157108 🎬 (01424) 307727 🚚
(01499) 083853 🛒 (01424) 317349 🍴 (01814) 233009 🔥 (01977) 059370 Ⴢ (01083) 272418 🔥
(01910) 854579 🔧 (01424) 501663 🔧 (01977) 776970 ⊠ (01814) 335222 ⊠ (01083) 278975 🛒
(01083) 051614 🔧 (01977) 677385 🛒 (01083) 175133 🔥 (01424) 020906 🔧 (01499) 858221 🍴
(01424) 082609 🔧 (01757) 083542 📚 (01860) 399246 🎬 (01860) 921375 ⊠ (01083) 247859 🍴
(01910) 220258 🛒 (01910) 681984 ✂ (01982) 208196 ✈ (01757) 437388 Ⴢ (01814) 029520 🏥
(01499) 774316 🔧 (01910) 623173 🎬 (01424) 062374 ✂ (01977) 540770 🍴 (01814) 927748 🎬
(01860) 963935 🏥 (01910) 461565 🛒 (01066) 752789 🎬 (01977) 561998 📚 (01066) 553647 🔧
(01814) 412816 🏥 (01083) 602444 🛒 (01977) 104103 🎬 (01814) 465861 🔧 (01977) 214378 🔧
(01977) 725473 ⊠ (01424) 651394 ✂ (01499) 790127 🔧 (01757) 292734 Ⴢ (01982) 217366 🔧
(01757) 673883 🔧 (01083) 837733 🔥 (01757) 494909 🍴 (01814) 999260 🎬 (01066) 591095 ⊠
(01499) 389866 ⊠ (01860) 561129 🛒 (01982) 887348 🏥 (01083) 677765 🔧 (01757) 277007 🎬
(01424) 813835 Ⴢ (01860) 212532 🔧 (01083) 989195 🔥 (01066) 578807 🛒 (01066) 576388 ✂
(01066) 044113 🍴 (01083) 267130 🚚 (01814) 670572 🎬 (01910) 766261 🔥 (01860) 510536 ✈

Answer [ ]

Question 6

How many *libraries* have the area code *(01734)*?

Key					
🏥 Hospitals	✈ Airports	▤ Libraries	🛒 Shops	✉ Post offices	🎞 Cinemas
🔥 Fire stations	🍴 Cafes	⊺ Bars	⚒ Repair shops	✂ Tailors	
🚢 Shipping companies	⚒ Plumbers				

(01777) 011111 🏥 (01734) 876208 🏥 (01862) 335908 🏥 (01426) 432258 ✈ (01734) 748552 ▤
(01260) 548745 🚢 (01230) 425443 🛒 (01159) 436259 ✉ (01765) 174961 🔥 (01734) 127434 ⚒
(01136) 576440 🛒 (01136) 606735 ✈ (01159) 512081 ✂ (01777) 448238 ✈ (01977) 075789 🚢
(01777) 142973 ✈ (01765) 909913 🔥 (01159) 149811 ✉ (01136) 723757 🏥 (01230) 513133 🔥
(01765) 009058 🔥 (01777) 599233 ▤ (01136) 581985 ✉ (01136) 612365 ✂ (01260) 876582 🎞
(01777) 011111 🏥 (01734) 876208 🏥 (01862) 335908 🏥 (01426) 432258 ✈ (01734) 748552 ▤
(01260) 548745 🚢 (01230) 425443 🛒 (01159) 436259 ✉ (01765) 174961 🔥 (01734) 127434 ⚒
(01136) 576440 🛒 (01136) 606735 ✈ (01159) 512081 ✂ (01777) 448238 ✈ (01977) 075789 🚢
(01777) 515318 🎞 (01159) 205300 🍴 (01862) 532325 🔥 (01765) 986370 ▤ (01426) 020802 🛒
(01159) 323521 ⚒ (01136) 078837 ✈ (01777) 726584 ✉ (01260) 609772 ▤ (01159) 691183 ⚒
(01862) 871236 ⚒ (01977) 536578 ✉ (01159) 204245 ▤ (01777) 908135 🛒 (01426) 624269 ⚒
(01734) 252565 ✉ (01136) 538754 🔥 (01136) 043413 ⚒ (01765) 128464 🚢 (01862) 363626 ✈
(01765) 778652 🎞 (01734) 796485 ✂ (01734) 530518 ▤ (01777) 172252 ▤ (01862) 970054 ⊺
(01159) 455615 🎞 (01136) 594221 🏥 (01260) 870953 ⚒ (01136) 403918 🎞 (01230) 305692 ✂
(01260) 353786 🚢 (01426) 802369 🎞 (01260) 673021 🏥 (01765) 365718 🔥 (01136) 517621 ✂
(01136) 944449 🚢 (01426) 340949 ⚒ (01777) 330410 ⊺ (01230) 461234 🚢 (01260) 370276 ⚒
(01734) 381891 🚢 (01426) 358852 ▤ (01765) 224979 🔥 (01777) 390023 ▤ (01862) 517246 🍴
(01426) 111755 🔥 (01734) 535839 ⚒ (01136) 016749 🛒 (01260) 182035 ⚒ (01159) 572740 ⚒
(01734) 090788 🏥 (01734) 659953 🔥 (01260) 653759 🛒 (01777) 376688 ⊺ (01862) 600723 🏥
(01777) 767200 ✂ (01977) 155830 ✂ (01426) 093815 🔥 (01765) 210122 🛒 (01136) 360474 ▤
(01777) 216473 ⚒ (01136) 361771 🏥 (01777) 452988 ▤ (01777) 446489 ⚒ (01777) 572311 🔥
(01159) 011350 ⊺ (01426) 844268 ⚒ (01977) 235134 🏥 (01136) 913737 ⊺ (01260) 051255 ⚒
(01777) 359804 🚢 (01230) 193099 ⊺ (01734) 246268 ⚒ (01159) 584879 🏥 (01734) 834895 🎞

Answer [　　　　　]

Question 7

How many **shops** have the area code *(01923)*?

Key

⊞	Hospitals	✈	Airports
▦	Libraries	🛒	Shops
⊠	Post offices	▣	Cinemas
🔥	Fire stations	🍴	Cafes
🍸	Bars	🔧	Repair shops
✂	Tailors	🚢	Shipping companies
🔧	Plumbers		

(01128) 480780 🍴 (01924) 644173 🍸 (01294) 690652 🍸 (01616) 706037 ✈ (01616) 012628 🔥
(01796) 163622 🚢 (01469) 129187 ✂ (01469) 753620 🔧 (01128) 731367 ▣ (01923) 448693 🛒
(01128) 293160 🔥 (01469) 565642 ▦ (01128) 597863 🔧 (01128) 205503 ▦ (01616) 480281 🛒
(01923) 168464 🔥 (01923) 015375 🛒 (01469) 457885 🔥 (01695) 833686 🛒 (01128) 215163 🔧
(01923) 315293 ⊠ (01294) 665652 🍸 (01616) 370530 🔧 (01616) 119828 ⊠ (01469) 653251 🚢
(01923) 502051 ⊞ (01294) 955642 🔧 (01469) 005719 ⊞ (01616) 995120 ▦ (01027) 912825 ▣
(01128) 798309 ⊞ (01237) 863797 ✂ (01027) 552395 ▦ (01027) 550040 🍴 (01128) 968382 🔥
(01027) 594678 🔧 (01027) 188310 ✈ (01237) 205201 ▣ (01294) 297561 ⊠ (01237) 472206 ✂
(01924) 497619 🍴 (01616) 281089 🔧 (01237) 077209 ▦ (01128) 838214 ⊞ (01923) 188512 ▣
(01027) 155585 🍴 (01616) 621743 🔥 (01796) 271386 🔥 (01924) 213436 🔧 (01294) 077163 🔧
(01796) 801085 🔧 (01616) 418738 ▦ (01923) 454064 🛒 (01616) 007344 🔧 (01128) 464630 ✂
(01128) 484888 🚢 (01796) 186256 ✈ (01237) 617363 🔧 (01695) 812596 🚢 (01796) 378197 ✂
(01237) 386737 🛒 (01616) 047823 🛒 (01237) 425173 🚢 (01469) 307488 🔧 (01128) 581276 ⊞
(01924) 668593 ▣ (01027) 074817 🚢 (01128) 615262 ⊞ (01027) 236535 ✂ (01796) 264120 ▣
(01924) 456119 ✂ (01695) 657686 ⊞ (01924) 562485 🛒 (01616) 035136 ⊠ (01695) 191592 🍸
(01294) 121049 🛒 (01128) 875516 🔥 (01237) 993272 🍴 (01796) 038114 🚢 (01924) 632387 ⊞
(01923) 322593 ▦ (01616) 887399 ▦ (01695) 563511 🔧 (01924) 941995 🛒 (01294) 473229 🍸
(01924) 351779 ✂ (01128) 196085 🔧 (01469) 375468 ✂ (01237) 877225 🍴 (01237) 563810 🛒
(01695) 725078 ▦ (01237) 661002 ✈ (01469) 889731 ✂ (01294) 341783 ▦ (01469) 234784 ✈
(01923) 920286 ⊞ (01469) 080672 🔥 (01924) 050719 🚢 (01616) 414769 ▣ (01923) 625542 ✈
(01695) 631691 🍸 (01923) 086436 🍸 (01294) 599615 🔧 (01027) 961156 ✈ (01616) 796845 🍴
(01027) 689423 🔧 (01796) 514287 ▣ (01923) 797454 🚢 (01616) 336967 ⊠ (01924) 660159 🚢
(01294) 726711 🍴 (01294) 515963 ▦ (01128) 500732 🍴 (01796) 116184 🔧 (01237) 370702 🔧

Answer [   ]

Question 8

How many **shipping companies** have the area code **(01662)**?

Key

📥 Hospitals	✈ Airports	📖 Libraries	🛒 Shops	✉ Post offices	🎦 Cinemas
🔥 Fire stations	🍴 Cafes	🍸 Bars	🔧 Repair shops	✂ Tailors	
🚚 Shipping companies	🔧 Plumbers				

(01479) 880910 ✈ (01211) 879429 📖 (01999) 937256 ✉ (01591) 660552 🍴 (01802) 442706 🔥
(01987) 038502 🔧 (01808) 712332 ✉ (01591) 035297 🎦 (01802) 074107 📥 (01987) 287200 🍸
(01808) 601501 🚚 (01987) 878843 📥 (01662) 019466 🚚 (01005) 550271 🛒 (01802) 169033 📖
(01999) 193014 ✂ (01479) 819197 ✂ (01211) 536284 🍸 (01591) 714557 🍸 (01808) 140913 🛒
(01808) 686558 ✈ (01987) 643850 🔥 (01005) 463653 🔥 (01662) 088544 📥 (01005) 089532 🚚
(01802) 198969 ✈ (01808) 281409 🎦 (01808) 888115 🔧 (01187) 240256 🔥 (01005) 323460 🎦
(01802) 613824 🔧 (01808) 121440 📖 (01808) 730183 🔥 (01662) 287250 🍸 (01999) 750269 ✉
(01999) 802331 🛒 (01187) 565045 ✈ (01662) 803587 🔧 (01808) 405003 🔧 (01999) 955798 📖
(01187) 078116 🔧 (01802) 287505 🎦 (01187) 676285 ✈ (01479) 617916 🛒 (01187) 789972 ✉
(01479) 340052 ✈ (01802) 235213 🔧 (01187) 327954 🍸 (01999) 763836 🍸 (01808) 275728 📥
(01999) 322745 📥 (01999) 658179 ✈ (01591) 976642 🍴 (01187) 140772 🛒 (01802) 802481 🔥
(01479) 332053 📥 (01999) 773167 🔧 (01591) 043193 📖 (01211) 452518 🎦 (01005) 376533 🔥
(01808) 336417 ✉ (01802) 410342 🍸 (01211) 899559 ✉ (01479) 462551 🔧 (01999) 503216 🍸
(01662) 539532 ✈ (01211) 167343 🔧 (01479) 476489 ✉ (01005) 065793 ✂ (01662) 598556 📥
(01808) 665303 🔥 (01187) 112668 🛒 (01591) 610580 📖 (01187) 654631 🍸 (01187) 215249 🚚
(01211) 509648 🍴 (01662) 247724 🚚 (01479) 544297 🔧 (01591) 935492 🚚 (01808) 807460 ✈
(01211) 348749 ✂ (01211) 226371 ✈ (01999) 406892 🛒 (01211) 923767 🛒 (01479) 282754 🚚
(01662) 527107 🔥 (01591) 264698 🔧 (01662) 160498 🔧 (01211) 743629 🚚 (01802) 387845 🛒
(01802) 102015 🎦 (01808) 841530 ✈ (01211) 731958 ✈ (01479) 315396 🔥 (01802) 620169 ✈
(01211) 882313 🔧 (01591) 360396 🔧 (01187) 410851 🍴 (01662) 837833 ✂ (01802) 211254 🔧

Answer [ ]

Question 9

Study the picture for 3 seconds, and then cover it up.

What did you see in the picture?

1. Cycle lane

2. Traffic lights showing red

3. A bike

4. A coach

5. Bus lane

Answer [   ]

Question 10

Study the picture for 3 seconds, and then cover it up.

What did you see in the picture?

1. A road sign

2. A car

3. A lamppost

4. A pedestrian

5. A Vauxhall garage

Answer

ANSWERS TO OBSERVATIONAL ABILITY TEST

Q1. A car, a cyclist.

Q2. Four cars, a road sign, a road junction.

Q3. 4

Q4. A motorway sign for junction 31, a caravan being towed, a lorry.

Q5. 2

Q6. 3

Q7. 3

Q8. 2.

Q9. A cycle lane, a coach.

Q10. A car, a lamppost.

CHAPTER 5

*Assessment
Centre Interview*

During the BTP assessment centre, you will normally be required to sit an interview. In some locations, you may be required to take an interview on another day, but generally you should expect to take the interview at the assessment centre. In some cases, you might also be asked to perform a presentation. If so, you will be provided details in your information pack, with which you will need to prepare thoroughly on the topic given to you.

The interview itself will be done in two parts:

-   The first part of the interview will be a *'get to know you'* interview, with the intention of assessing your motivations and reasons for applying to the Transport Police. The interviewers are highly likely to ask you questions based around the personal statement from your original application form, so make sure you know this off by heart.

-   The second part of the interview will be based around the core competencies. For example, you might have to explain how you have resolved a particular situation using the STAR method. You'll need to show a clear understanding of all the requirements of the job role, and demonstrate that you can apply these to a high standard.

Whilst you will be nervous, you should try not to let this get in the way of your success. British Transport Police Officers, in general, are confident people who have the ability to rise to a challenge and perform in difficult and pressurised situations. Treat the interview no differently to this. You ARE capable of joining the British Transport Police and the nerves that you have on the day are only natural, in fact they will help you to perform better if you have prepared sufficiently.

The crucial element to your success is your preparation. The interviewers will have a number of set questions to choose from and, whilst these are constantly changing, they are specifically designed to assess the police officer core competencies. Before attending your interview, ensure that you read, digest and understand the Transport Police core competencies. Without these it will be very difficult to pass the interview.

BTP ASSESSMENT CENTRE: INITIAL INTERVIEW QUESTIONS

In the build-up to your interview, you need to think carefully about why you want to become a police officer, and what it is exactly that has attracted you to the role. Candidates who want to become a police officer so that they can *'catch criminals'* and *'ride about on trains all day'* will score poorly. Only you will know the exact reasons why you want to join the BTP, but here are some examples of strong and weak responses.

Strong reasons:

- To make a difference to railways, make rail transport safer and reduce any fear that the public may have;

- To carry out a job that is worthwhile and makes a difference;

- The different challenges that you will face on a day-to-day basis;

- The chance to work with a highly professional team that is committed to achieving the values and principles of the service;

- The opportunity to learn new skills.

After studying this guide, you will know a considerable amount about the role of a Transport Police Officer. Remember that the role is predominantly based around the core competencies, so make sure you are familiar with them before you attend the interview. It is also advisable that you study your recruitment literature and the website of the BTP.

During the final interview there is a strong possibility that you will be asked questions that relate to the BTP itself.

The following sample questions are the types of questions that have been asked during final interviews in the past:

Q. What is it that has attracted you to the BTP?

Q. What can you tell me about the structure of the BTP?

Q. Can you tell me how the BTP is doing in relation to rail crime reduction?

Q. What crime reduction activities is the BTP currently involved in?

Q. Who are our partners and stakeholders?

In order to prepare for questions that relate to the BTP, your first port of call is their website. From here you will be able to find out a considerable amount of information about their structure, their activities and their success in driving down crime.

You may also wish to consider contacting your local police station and asking if it is possible to talk to a serving police officer about his or her role and the activities that the service are currently engaged in.

Below we have included some examples of the most common type of questions you should expect to see in the first part of your interview. We've also created some model answers to these questions, to give you a better idea of how to respond.

Sample Question 1

Tell us why you want to become a Transport Police Officer?

Sample response

"I have worked in my current role now for a number of years. I have an excellent employer, and enjoy working for them, but unfortunately no longer find my job challenging.

I understand that the role of a Transport Police Officer is both demanding and rewarding, and I believe that I have the qualities to thrive in such an environment. I love working under pressure, working as part of a team that is diverse in nature and helping people in difficult situations.

Rail customer expectations of the Transport Police are very high and I believe that I have the right qualities to help deliver a great service to the public. I have studied the police core competencies and believe that I have the skills to match them and deliver what they require."

Things to consider:

- Don't be negative about your current or previous employer;
- Be positive, enthusiastic and upbeat in your response;
- Make reference to the core competencies if possible.

Sample Question 2

Why have you chosen the British Transport Police?

Sample response

"I have carried out extensive research into the British Transport Police, and I have been impressed by the level of service it provides. Your website provides the community with direct access to a different range of topics and the work that is being carried out on railways across the country is very impressive.

I have looked at the national and local railway crime statistics and read many different newspapers and articles. The officers that I have spoken to have told me that they get a great deal of job satisfaction from working for the Transport Police."

Things to consider:

- Research the BTP thoroughly and make reference to particular success stories;

- Be positive, enthusiastic and upbeat in your response;

- Be positive about the service and don't be critical of it, even if you think it needs improving in certain areas.

Sample Question 3

What does the role of a Transport Police Officer involve?

Sample response

"Prior to my application, I viewed Transport Police Officers as people who simply caught fare dodgers, and worked to reduce crime. After undertaking a great deal of research, I can now see that the role of a Transport Police Officer is far more diverse and varied. For example, they are there to serve the community and reduce the element of fear. They do this by communicating with rail passengers and being visual wherever possible. They may need to pay particular attention to a person or groups of people who are the victims of crime or hatred.

Therefore the role of a Transport Police Officer is to both physically and psychologically protect the rail community that they are serving. It is also their role to work with other organisations such as Transport for London and other public sector bodies to try to reduce crime in a co-ordinated response."

Things to consider:

- Understand the Transport Police core competencies and be able to recite them word for word.

Sample Question 4

If one of your team members discussed their sexual preferences with you over a cup of tea at work, how do you think you would react?

Sample response

"I would have no problem at all. A person's sexual preference is their right and they should not be treated any differently for this. My attitude towards them and our working relationship would not be affected in any way. I have always treated everyone with respect and dignity at all times and will continue to do so throughout my career."

Things to consider:

- Understand everything there is to know about equality and fairness. If you do not believe in equality, then this job is not for you;

- Visit the website http://www.thelgbtnetwork.org.uk.

Sample Question 5

If you were given an order that you thought was incorrect, would you carry it out?

Sample response

"Yes I would. I would always respect my senior officers and their decisions. However, if I thought something could be done in a better way, then I do think that it is important to put this across, but in a structured and non-confrontational manner. The most appropriate time to offer up my opinions and views would be during debrief, but I would never refuse to carry out an order or even question it during an operational incident."

Sample Question 6

What do you understand by the term equality and fairness?

Sample response

"It is an unfortunate fact that certain groups in society are still more likely to suffer from unfair treatment and discrimination than others. It is important that the British Transport Police and its staff strive to eliminate all forms of unfair treatment and discrimination, on the grounds that are specified in their policies or codes of practice. Equality and fairness is the working culture in which fair treatment of all is the norm."

Things to consider:

- Try to read the BTP policy on equality and fairness. You may be able to find this by visiting their website or asking them for a copy of it to help you in your preparation;

- Consider reading the Race Relations Act, and understand the duties that are placed upon public sector organisations such as the Transport Police.

Sample Question 7

"How do you think the Transport Police could recruit more people from ethnic minority groups?"

Sample response

"To begin with, it is important that the BTP continue to build effective public relations. This can be achieved through certain avenues such as the service's website or even the local press. If the BTP has a community liaison officer, then this would be a good way to break down any barriers in the communities that we want to recruit from. Another option is to ask people from these specific groups how they view the Transport Police, and what they think we could do to recruit more people from their community."

Comprehensive list of initial interview questions to prepare for:

Q. *Why do you want to become a Transport Police Officer?*

Q. *What are your strengths?*

Q. *What are your weaknesses?*

Q. *What do you understand by the term 'teamwork'?*

Q. *What makes an effective team?*

Q. *Why would you make a good Transport Police Officer?*

Q. *What do you think the role of a Transport Police Officer entails?*

Q. *If you saw a colleague being bullied or harassed, what would you do?*

Q. *What do you think the qualities of an effective Transport Police Officer are?*

Q. *What have you done so far to find out about the role of a Transport Police Officer?*

Q. *Give examples of when you have had to work as part of a team.*

Q. *What would you do if a member of your team was not pulling their weight or doing their job effectively?*

Q. *Have you ever had to diffuse a confrontational situation? What did you do and what did you say?*

Q. *What are the main issues effecting the Transport Police at this current time?*

Q. What do you understand about the term 'equality and fairness'?

Q. What do you understand by the term 'equal opportunities'?

Q. If you ever heard a racist or sexist remark, what would you do?

Q. Would you say that you are a motivated person?

Q. How do you keep yourself motivated?

Q. Have you ever had to work as part of a team to achieve a common goal?

Q. Have you ever made a poor decision? If so, what was it?

Q. If you were ever given an order that you thought was incorrect, what would you do?

Q. Have you ever had to work with somebody that you dislike?

Q. Have you ever carried out a project from beginning to end?

Q. How do you think you would cope with anti-social working hours?

Q. Have you ever had to work shifts?

BRITISH TRANSPORT POLICE ASSESSMENT CENTRE: COMPETENCY BASED QUESTIONS

The second part of the interview will last for up to 20 minutes. You will be asked several questions about how you have previously dealt with specific situations. These questions will be related to the competency areas relevant to the role of a British Transport Police Officer, which can be found in the information pack. You will be given 5 minutes to answer each question, and will be stopped if you go over this time limit. The person interviewing you may also provide you with a written copy of the question to refer to when answering. You should be prepared to answer further questions, in order to deliver a full response.

The interviewer will assess your responses against the type of behaviours that you will need to exhibit, whilst working as a Transport Police Officer. You must make sure that you are familiar with the competencies and that your answer gives you an opportunity to explain how you have shown this behaviour.

They will assess you on five different competencies during the interview. *Oral communication* will be assessed throughout the interview, and you will be asked one question in relation to the following **four** competency areas:

- *Service Delivery;*
- *Serving the Public;*
- *Professionalism;*
- *Working with Others.*

PREPARING FOR THE ASSESSMENT CENTRE INTERVIEW

When preparing for the interview you should try to formulate responses to questions that demonstrate the core competencies.

The responses that you provide should include specific examples of what you have done in particular scenarios. In your 'welcome pack', which will be sent to you approximately 2 weeks before the date of your assessment centre, you should find examples of the 'core competencies' that are relevant to a Transport Police Officer. These are the criteria that you will be scored against, so it is worthwhile reading them beforehand and trying to structure your answers around them as best you can.

For example, one of the sections you will be assessed against could be *'working with others'*. You may be asked to *'give an example of where you worked effectively as part of a team, in order to achieve a difficult task or goal'.* Try to structure your answer around the core competencies required, e.g. you worked cooperatively with the others involved, supported the rest of the team members and persuaded them to follow your ideas in order to complete the task. Do not fall into the trap of providing a 'generic' response that details what you 'would do' if the situation arose, unless of course you have not been in this type of situation before.

When responding to situational questions, try to structure your responses in a logical and concise manner. The way to achieve this is to use the '**STAR**' method:

Situation

Start off your response to the interview question by explaining what the 'situation' was and who was involved.

Task

Once you have detailed the situation, explain what the 'task' was, or what needed to be done.

Action

Now explain what 'action' you took, and what action others took. Also explain why you took this particular course of action.

Result

Explain to the panel what you would do differently if the same situation arose again. It is good to be reflective at the end of your responses. This demonstrates a level of maturity and it will also show the panel that you are willing to learn from every experience.

Finally, explain what the outcome or result was following your actions. Try to demonstrate in your response that the result was positive because of the action that you took.

On the following page I have provided you with an example of how your response could be structured if you were responding to a question that was based around the core competency of *professionalism*. Remember that the following sample question and response is for <u>example purposes only</u>.

Sample interview question – (professionalism)

Please provide an example of where you have taken responsibility to resolve a problem?

"After reading a newspaper appeal from a local children's charity, I decided to try and raise money for this worthwhile cause by organising a charity car wash day at the local school during the summer holidays. I decided that the event would take place in a month's time, which would give me enough time to organise things. The head teacher at the school agreed to support me during the organisation of the event and provide me with the necessary resources required to make it a success.

I set about organising the event, but soon realised that I had made a mistake in trying to arrange everything on my own. I arranged for two of my work colleagues to assist me. Once they had agreed to help me, I started out by providing them with a brief of what I wanted them to do. I informed them that, in order for the event to be a success, we needed to act with integrity and professionalism at all times.

I asked one of them to organise the booking of the school and to arrange local sponsorship in the form of buckets, sponges and car wash soap to use on the day, so that we did not have to use our own personal money to buy them. I asked the second person to arrange advertising in the local newspaper and radio stations so that we could let the local community know about our charity car wash event, which would in turn hopefully bring in more money for the charity.

Following a successful advertising campaign, I was inundated with calls from local newspapers about our event, and it was becoming hard work to keep talking to them and explaining what the event was all about. However, I knew that this information was important if we were to raise our target of £500.

Everything was going well right up to the morning of the event, when I realised we had not picked up the key to open the school gates. It was during the summer holidays, so the caretaker was not there to open the gates for us. Not wanting to let everyone down, I jumped in my car, made my way down to the caretaker's house and managed to wake him up and get the key just in time before the car wash event was due to start. In the end the day was a great success and we managed to raise £600 for the local charity. Throughout the event I put in lots of extra effort in order to make it a great success.

Once the event was over, I decided to ask the head teacher for feedback on how he thought I had managed the project. He provided me with some excellent feedback and some good pointers for how I might improve in the future when organising events. I took on board this feedback in order to improve my skills."

Now that we have taken a look at a sample response, let's explore how the response matched the core competency.

How the response matches the core competency being assessed:

In order to demonstrate how effective the above response is, I have broken it down into sections and provided the core competency area that it matches.

"...I decided to try to raise money for this worthwhile cause by organising a charity car wash day..."

Core competency matched:

- Acts with integrity.
- Uses own initiative.

"Once they had agreed to help me, I started out by providing them with a brief of what I wanted them to do. I informed them that, in order for the event to be a success, we needed to act with integrity and professionalism at all times."

Core competency matched:

- Acting with integrity.
- Demonstrating a strong work ethic.

"...which would give me enough time to organise such an event."

Core competency matched:

- Takes ownership.

"I set about organising the event and soon realised that I had made a mistake in trying to arrange everything on my own, so I arranged for 2 of my work colleagues to assist me."

Core competency matched:

- Takes ownership.
- Uses initiative.

> *"…arrange local sponsorship in the form of buckets, sponges and car wash soap to use on the day, so that we did not have to use our own personal money to buy them."*

Core competency matched:

- Uses initiative.

> *"Once the event was over I decided to ask the head teacher for feedback on how he thought I had managed the project. He provided me with some excellent feedback and some good pointers for how I might improve in the future when organising events. I took on-board this feedback in order to improve my skills."*

Core competency matched:

- Asks for and acts on feedback.

> *"Following a successful advertising campaign, I was inundated with calls from local newspapers about our event and it was becoming hard work to keep talking to them and explaining what the event was all about. But I knew that this information was important if we were to raise our target of £500."*

Core competency matched:

- Uses initiative.

"Not wanting to let everyone down, I jumped in my car, made my way down to the caretaker's house and managed to wake him up and get the key just in time before the car wash event was due to start."

Core competency matched:

- Uses initiative.
- Takes ownership.
- Showing a strong work ethic.

The explanations above have hopefully highlighted the importance of matching the core competencies that are being assessed.

- On the following pages, I have provided you with a number of sample interview questions that are based around the core competencies.

- Following each question, we have provided you with some useful tips and advice on how you may consider answering the question.

- Once you have read the question and the tips, use the template on the following page to create a response using your own experiences and knowledge.

Interview Question 1 - *(Working with Others)*

Please provide an example of where you have worked as part of a team to achieve a difficult task.

TOP TIPS!

Helpful Tips

- Try to think of a situation where you volunteered to work as part of a team in order to achieve a difficult task. It is better to say that you volunteered as opposed to being asked to get involved by another person.

- Candidates who can provide an example of where they achieved the task, despite the constraints of time, will generally score better.

Consider structuring your response in the following manner:

Step 1: Explain what the situation was and how you became involved.

Step 2: Now explain who else was involved and what the task was.

Step 3: Explain why the task was difficult and whether there were any time constraints.

Step 4: Explain how it was decided who would carry out that task.

Step 5: Now explain what had to be done and how you overcame any obstacles or hurdles.

Step 6: Explain what the result/outcome was. Try to make the result sound positive as a consequence of your actions.

Now use the template on the following page to construct your own response to this question, based on your own experiences and knowledge

---

Sample competency based interview question 1

Please provide an example of where you have worked as part of a team to perform a difficult task

Sample competency based interview question 2 – *(Professionalism)*

Provide an example of where you have challenged discriminatory or inappropriate behaviour. What did you do and what did you say?

TOP TIPS!

- Study the core competency that relates to respect for race and diversity before constructing your response.

- When challenging this type of behaviour, make sure that you remain calm at all times and never become aggressive or confrontational.

Consider structuring your response in the following manner:

Step 1: Explain what the situation was and how you became involved.

Step 2: Now explain who else was involved, and why you felt that the behaviour was inappropriate or discriminatory. What was it that was being said or done?

Step 3: Now explain what you said or did and why.

Step 4: Explain how the other person/people reacted when you challenged the behaviour.

Step 5: Now explain what the end result was. Try to make it sound like the result was positive because of your actions.

Step 6: Finally, explain why you think it was that the people/person behaved as they did.

Now use the template on the following page to construct your own response to this question based on your own experiences and knowledge.

Sample competency based interview question 2

Provide an example of where you have challenged discriminatory or inappropriate behaviour. What did you do and what did you say?

Sample competency based interview question 3 - *(Working with Others)*

Provide an example of where you have helped somebody from a different culture or background to your own. What did you do and what did you say?

TOP TIPS!

- Study the core competency that relates to respect for race and diversity before constructing your response.

- Try to think of a situation where you have gone out of your way to help somebody.

- Try to use keywords and phrases from the core competency in your response.

Consider structuring your response in the following manner:

Step 1: Explain what the situation was and how you became involved. It is better to say that you volunteered to be involved rather than to say that you were asked to.

Step 2: Now explain who else was involved, and why they needed your help or assistance.

Step 3: Now explain what you said or did and why. Also explain any factors you took into consideration when helping them.

Step 4: Explain how the other person/people reacted to your help or assistance. Did they benefit from it?

Step 5: Now explain what the end result was. Try to make the result sound positive following your actions.

Now use the template below to construct your own response to this question based on your own experiences and knowledge.

Sample competency based interview question 3

Provide an example of where you have helped somebody from a different culture or background to your own. What did you do and what did you say?

Sample competency based interview question4 - *(Professionalism)*

Provide an example of where you have solved a difficult problem. What did you do?

TOP TIPS!

- Study the core competency that relates to problem solving.

- Try to include keywords and phrases from the core competency in your response to this question.

Consider structuring your response in the following manner:

Step 1: Explain what the situation was and why the problem was difficult.

Step 2: Now explain what action you took in order to solve the difficult problem.

Step 3: Now explain why you took that particular action, and also the thought process behind your actions.

Step 4: Explain the barriers or difficulties that you had to overcome.

Step 5: Now explain what the end result was. Try to make the result sound positive as a result of your actions.

Now use the template on the following page to construct your own response to this question based on your own experiences and knowledge.

Sample competency based interview question 4

Provide an example of where you have solved a difficult problem. What did you do?

Sample competency based interview question 5 - (*Serving the Public*)

Provide an example of where you have broken down barriers between a group of people?

TOP TIPS!

- Study the core competency that relates to serving the public.

- Try to include keywords and phrases from the core competency in your response to this question, such as: *"I tried to understand each person's needs and concerns"* , *"I took steps to identify the best way that we could all work together"*, *"I had their best interests at heart throughout"*, *"I built confidence in them by talking to them."*

Consider structuring your response in the following manner:

Step 1: Explain what the situation was and why you needed to break down the barriers.

Step 2: Now explain what steps you took in order to achieve the goal.

Step 3: Now explain why you took that particular action, and also the thought process behind your actions.

Step 4: Explain the barriers or difficulties that you had to overcome in order to achieve the task/objective.

Step 5: Now explain what the end result was. Try to make the result sound positive following your actions.

Now use the template on the following page to construct your own response to this question, based on your own experiences and knowledge.

Sample competency based interview question 5

Provide an example of where you have broken down barriers between a group of people?

Sample competency based interview question 6 - *(Service Delivery)*

Please provide an example of where you have organised a difficult task effectively?

TOP TIPS!

- Carefully read the core competency that relates to service delivery.

- Try to include keywords and phrases from the core competency in your response to this question.

Consider structuring your response in the following manner:

Step 1: Explain what the situation was and what it was you needed to organise.

Step 2: Now explain why the task was so difficult.

Step 3: Now explain what you did and why you did it. Also explain your considerations when organising the task.

Step 4: Explain what problems you had and how you overcame them.

Step 5: Finally explain what the end result was. Try to provide a positive outcome to the situation.

Now use the template on the following page to construct your own response to this question, based on your own experiences and knowledge.

Sample competency based interview question 6

Please provide an example of where you have organised a difficult task effectively?

Sample competency based interview question 7 - *(Professionalism)*

Tell me about a time when you changed how you did something, in response to feedback from someone else?

> **TOP TIPS!**   *Helpful Tips*
>
> • What did you need to develop?
>
> • What feedback did you receive and from whom?
>
> • What steps did you take to improve yourself or someone else?
>
> • What did you specifically say or do?
>
> • What was the end result?

Strong candidates:

Transport Police Officers receive feedback from their supervisory managers on a regular basis. In their quest to continually improve, the Police Service will invest time, finances and resources into your development. Part of the learning process includes being able to accept feedback and also being able to improve as a result of it. Strong candidates will be able to provide specific examples of where they have taken feedback from an employer or otherwise, and used it to improve themselves.

Weak candidates:

Candidates who are unable to accept and use feedback from others will generally provide a weak response to this type of question. They will fail to grasp the importance of feedback and in particular where it lies in relation to continuous improvement. Their response will be generic in nature and there will be no real substance or detail to their answer.

Now take the time to prepare your own response to this question.

Sample competency based interview question 7

Tell me about a time when you changed how you did something, in response to feedback from someone else?

More sample questions to prepare for, based on the assessable core competencies

In this section I will provide you with a number of sample interview questions to prepare for.

SERVICE DELIVERY

Q. Give an example of when you have worked towards an organisation's objectives and/or priorities?

Q. Give an example of when you have planned and organised a difficult task.

Q. Give an example of when you have carried out many different tasks at once.

Q. Give an example of when you have sought advice from others whilst carrying out a difficult work-related task.

SERVING THE PUBLIC

Q. Give an example of when you have provided excellent customer service.

Q. Give an example of when you have addressed someone else's needs or expectations.

Q. Give an example of when you have broken down barriers amongst a group of people.

Q. Give an example of when you have worked with another person or group of people to deliver an excellent level of service.

PROFESSIONALISM

Q. Give an example of when you have worked in accordance with an organisation's standards or ethics.

Q. Give an example of when you have taken ownership of a particular problem.

Q. Give an example of when you have acted on your own initiative to resolve an issue or difficult problem.

Q. Give an example of when you have challenged discriminatory or inappropriate behaviour.

Q. Give an example of when you have acted on feedback which has been supplied by someone else.

Q. Give an example of when you have resolved a difficult situation in a calm manner.

Q. Give an example of when you have defused a potentially hostile situation.

WORKING WITH OTHERS

Q. Give an example of when you have supported other members of a team.

Q. Give an example of when you have worked with other people to achieve a difficult task.

Q. Give an example of when you have briefed a team in relation to a difficult task which had to be achieved.

Q. Give an example of when you have persuaded a group of people to follow your course of action or plan.

How to improve your scores through effective oral communication

Whilst you will not normally be questioned directly in relation to oral communication, you will be assessed indirectly.

Consider the following points in regards to your interview:

- When you walk into the interview room, stand up straight and introduce yourself. Be polite and courteous at all times and try to come across in a pleasant manner. The panel will be assessing you as soon as you walk through the door, so make sure that you give a positive first impression.

- Do not sit down in the interview chair until you are invited to do so - this is good manners.

- When you sit down in the interview chair, sit up straight and do not fidget or slouch. It is acceptable to use hand gestures when explaining your responses to the questions but don't overdo it, as they can become a distraction.

- Structure your responses to the questions in a logical manner – this is very important. When responding to an interview question, start at the beginning and work your way through in a concise manner, and at a pace that is easy for the panel to listen to.

- Speak clearly and in a tone that is easy for the panel to hear. Be confident in your responses.

- When talking to the panel, use eye contact, but be careful not to look at them in an intimidating manner.

- Consider wearing some form of formal outfit to the interview such as a suit. Whilst you will not be assessed on the type of outfit that you wear to the interview, it will make you come across in a more professional manner.

TOP TIPS!

- Always provide 'specific' examples to the questions being asked.

- During your responses try to outline your contributions and also provide evidence of the competency area that is being assessed.

- Speak clearly, use correct English and structure your responses in a logical and concise manner.

- Carry out a mock interview prior to your actual interview day.

- When answering your questions, respond to the whole panel and not just the person asking you the question.

- Make eye contact with the members of the panel as opposed to looking at the floor.

- Rest the palms of your hands on your knees when you are not using them to express yourself and keep your feet flat on the ground.

You may find some of the following phrases useful when constructing your answers:

Dignity and respect	Team working and working with others	Strong working relationships	Effective team member
Achieving common goals	Customer focus	Public service	Resilient
Community policing	Sensitive to cultural issues	Sensitive towards racial differences	Presenting the right image to the public
Effective communication	Identify problems and make effective decisions	Motivated, conscientious and committed	Calm, considerate and can work well under pressure

CHAPTER 6

Fitness & Vetting

The final stage of the British Transport Police assessment centre is the fitness test. Depending on the geographical area in which you are applying, this will either take place directly after the interview (on the same day), or at a later date.

In order to successfully join the BTP, it is essential that you can display a good level of fitness. Similarly to Police Officers, there are times when Transport Police Officers may be required to deal with offenders in a physical manner, and may even have to give chase! To do this, you'll need have a great level of physical fitness, and will need to maintain this fitness throughout your career in the British Transport Police.

The BTP fitness test consists of 2 stages. These are the **Dynamic Strength Test** and the **Endurance Fitness Test**. *You will need to meet the minimum standard in both of these tests in order to be successful.* If you do fail any parts of the test on your first attempt, then you will be allowed three reattempts. In the event that your reattempts are unsuccessful, you will be unable to reapply for a period of six months. If you are successful, then you should expect to be assessed on a regular basis to ensure that you are maintaining your levels of fitness.

The Dynamic Strength Test

The Dynamic Strength Test requires you to perform five chest pushes (whilst seated) and five back pulls (whilst seated) on a Dyno Machine. Your performance will be measured against the average force of your pushes and pulls.

In the **chest pushing** exercise, you will sit with your back against the padding of the Dyno Machine, and your feet flat on the floor. You will perform 3 warmups, followed by 5 pushes. There will be a 3 second period of recovery between each push. In order to pass the chest pushing exercise, you'll need to push an average of 34kg.

In the chest pulling exercise you will sit with your chest against the padding of the Dyno Machine, and your feet flat on the floor. You will perform 3 warmups, followed by 5 pulls. There will be a 3 second period of recovery between each pull. In order to pass the chest pulling exercise, you will need to pull an average of 35kg.

The Endurance Fitness Test

The Endurance Fitness Test will require you to run back and forth between 2 points on a 15 metre track, in time with a number of verbal bleeps. The timing between these bleeps will gradually decrease i.e. get faster, the longer the test goes on.

Candidates are required to run until they can no longer reach the other end of the track before the next bleep. In order to pass the Fitness Test, you will need to reach Level 5. While this might sound intimidating, with the right preparation, Level 5 is actually fairly easy to reach.

In the build up to the Endurance Fitness Test, I recommend taking part in regular sporting activities, such as football or tennis. This will improve your aerobic fitness, which in turn will lend to your ability to pass the Fitness Test.

Vetting & Medical

Following the fitness test, you will face a short wait to find out whether you have been successful. If you are successful, you'll receive a **conditional** offer from the BTP. This offer is subject to a number of pre-employment checks, that the BTP will run to make sure that you are suitable for the position.

You will be checked thoroughly via vetting and national security vetting. What this means is that you'll be examined by both internal police constabularies, and external security forces. As we mentioned earlier in the guide, your family background and relatives will also be closely examined, to ensure you are suitable.

You'll then be invited to attend a medical, where you will be subject to a number of different physical checks. In particular, the BTP will pay close attention to your eyesight.

In order to pass the BTP eyesight test, you'll need to demonstrate the following:

- **Distance Vision.** You will need to demonstrate that you are 6/12 with 1 eye, or 6/6 with both eyes. Applicants who wear glasses or contact lenses will need to reach a level of 6/36 without your glasses or contacts.

- **Near Vision.** 6/9 with both eyes used together.

- **Colour Vision.** You will need healthy colour vision to apply. If you are someone who needs colour correcting lenses or glasses, you will be unable to apply.

Training

If you successfully pass the medical, then congratulations, you will have gained a place with the British Transport Police. What follows is an intense, 24 month probationary period, where you will learn how to handle yourself in the role. This probationary period is separated into three different stages:

Stage 1: Training

The first stage is a rigorous 21 week training course, broken down into a series of modules and tests. During your first week of training, you'll need to sit the Endurance Fitness Test again. Then, the rest of your training will consist of module based learning, examinations, safety training, role play exercises and a community placement.

Stage 2: Tutoring

The next stage is the tutoring stage. During this period, you will be assigned a mentor, who you will pair up with for operational patrols. This will take place over an 8 week period, and will allow you to put everything you have learned so far, into practice.

Stage 3: Practical Learning

During the final 72 week period, you will be required to maintain a portfolio which demonstrates how you have met the standards needed for a Level 3 Diploma in Policing Practice.

During the final week of your training, you will be required to attend a final assessment programme, which can last for up to a week. If you successfully pass this, then you will be recognised as a fully qualified British Transport Police Officer, and your probationary period will be finished.

CHAPTER 7

A Few Final Words

You have now reached the end of the guide and no doubt will be ready to start preparing for the British Transport Police selection process. The majority of candidates who pass the selection process have a number of common attributes.

These are as follows:

1. They believe in themselves.

The first factor is self-belief. Regardless of what anyone tells you, you can become a Transport Police Officer. Just like any job of this nature, you have to be prepared to work hard in order to be successful. Make sure that you have the self-belief to pass the selection process and fill your mind with positive thoughts.

2. They prepare fully.

The second factor is preparation. Those people who achieve in life prepare fully for every eventuality and that is what you must do when you apply to become a Transport Police Officer. Work very hard and especially concentrate on your weak areas.

3. They persevere.

Perseverance is a fantastic word. Everybody comes across obstacles or setbacks in their life, but it is what you do about those setbacks that is important. If you fail at something, then consider *'why'* you have failed. This will allow you to improve for next time and if you keep improving and trying, success will eventually follow. Apply this same method of thinking when you apply to join the BTP.

4. They are self-motivated.

How much do you want this job? Do you want it, or do you really want it? When you apply to join the BTP, you should want it more than anything in the world. Your levels of self-motivation will shine through on your application and during your interview. For the weeks and months leading up to the selection process, try to stay as motivated as you can, and always keep your fitness levels up.

Work hard, stay focused and you can achieve anything that you set your mind to!

Attend a 1-day Police Officer course run by former Police Officers at: **www.PoliceCourse. co.uk**